Mr Mike Pender
8 Friars Way
London ON N6G 2A8

D0966290

FEAR AND
LOATHING IN
LOCHGELLY

Fear and Loathing in Lochgelly

RON FERGUSON

Northern Books
from Famedram

From the same author:

Hitler was a Vegetarian

Donald Dewar ate my Hamster

Black Diamonds and the Blue Brazil

Geoff: the Life of Geoffrey M Shaw

ISBN 0905489 77 2
© *Copyright 2003 Ron Ferguson and* The Herald

Published by Famedram Publishers Ltd AB41 9EA
www.northernbooks.co.uk

Printed by Thomson Press (I) Ltd
C35 Phase II Noida

Contents

Foreword

Ron Ferguson is unusual. He is an unusual newspaper columnist not least because everyone likes him. Not everyone agrees with him, as the correspondence columns of *The Herald* and his own post-bag bear eloquent testimony, but I have never known anyone to offer a bad word about him personally.

He has come to the columnar art by an unusual route. From Cowdenbeath to Kierkegaard by way of Easterhouse and Iona is certainly an unconventional path to travel, but Ron's keen observations and rich experiences along the way are what gives these columns and his other writing their great charm and humanity.

Perhaps that is why he is capable of provoking an unusually broad range of responses. Many columnists have the knowledge and skill to teach us things we did not know about the world we share, but few like Ron possess that rare gift of teaching us things about ourselves.

Like the gifted footballer cursed with the accolade of being the best player never to represent his country, Ron, one of the finest preachers of his generation, has often been referred to as the best minister never to be Moderator. But his columns never sermonise. Rather, with the intimacy normally reserved for close friendship, he has the uncanny ability of articulating the emotions few have the talent to put into words.

When you have finished reading this worthy successor to *Donald Dewar Ate my Hamster* and *Hitler was a Vegetarian*, two things will have happened. You will have laughed out loud. You will also have found yourself questioning views you previously regarded as immutable..... occasionally at the same time. An unusual combination indeed.

COLIN MCDIARMID
Executive Editor,
The Herald.

Introduction

Leslie Stephen, founder of the National Dictionary of Biography and father of Virginia Woolf, once sneered that journalism was the business of "writing for pay about matters of which you are ignorant". Many people would believe that that is a particularly apt description of the art of the columnist.

They are right, of course. Columns are all about opinions, and columnists often stray into territories in which their grasp of the terrain is somewhat less than secure. On almost every subject the columnist writes about, there will be readers who are expert. They usually feel it their public duty to point out the writer's ignorance, and they are right to do so. Argument is the lifeblood of newspapers.

The columnist is a high-wire artist who takes a weekly or bi-weekly walk high in the big top, without a safety net. His or her job is to challenge, to illumine, to annoy, to inspire, to provoke, to entertain. When the columnist ceases to do that, the pay cheque ceases to drop through the letterbox and the cornflakes are no longer on the table.

Writing for *The Herald* is a pleasure. The response of readers, often affirmative, sometimes critical, always adding to my own knowledge, makes it a weekly conversation of delight. Writing opinions for money is a great privilege, and I am most of all grateful to the *Herald* readers, without whom I would have no audience and no money.

I would like to thank Mark Douglas-Home, editor of the *Herald,* for his encouragement, as well as for permission to reproduce these pieces. Particular thanks are due to Colin McDiarmid, the paper's Executive Editor, not only for writing the foreword to this collection, but for the stimulation of our weekly conversations about the subject matter of the column. Thanks also to Orkney's Bill McArthur, Scotland's highly regarded Cartoonist of the Year, for his – as usual – high quality illustrations. And a big thank-you to Famedram's Bill Williams for so enthusiastically publishing this third book of columns.

I am grateful also to Hunter S. Thompson for his cult classic *Fear and Loathing in Las Vegas.* Lochgelly may not be quite so exotic as LA, but it has its own style. Lochgelly post office has two openings for letters, one marked "Lochgelly" and the other "The rest of the world". I like that.

RON FERGUSON

Princess Di, This is Your After-life

So, Princess Di is enjoying herself in the afterlife. Good on her. According to psychics, the Princess of Wales is "having fun", and is spending time with Mother Teresa. Whether they are both whooping it up at heavenly raves hasn't been revealed.

Where does all this stuff come from? Celebrity television, of course. The programme, *Spirit of Diana*, was shown on a pay-per-view US channel. Viewers had to pay to watch the séance, much as they would to watch a big football match. Presumably there were slow-motion replays, and commentators.

On the show, two British mediums, Craig and Jane Hamilton-Parker, claimed to have contacted the princess. Just as well. It would have been somewhat disappointing for the viewers who had paid up front if the reception had been bad – a bit like paying £30 to see a live world boxing title fight and watching Mike Tyson being knocked out in the first 15 seconds.

But, trouper that she is, Diana showed up. Never misses a photo opportunity in her afterlife either.

"It was a wonderful link," said Mrs Parker-Bowles, I mean Hamilton-Parker. "It was very, very real. She was getting excited. She found it all rather amusing."

As one does. Especially when one is in heaven: where, it seems, there are shops.

During the séance, apparently, Diana kept changing her clothes – from casual trousers to a denim blouse, and then to suits. The princess, it seems, has a big wardrobe in heaven. I hope the British taxpayers are not paying for all this.

The psychics claim the princess, who was looking well – that's nice – told them she had definitely planned to marry Dodi al Fayed. Well, that solves that one. "Fuggin' right, it does," as the phoney pharaoh, Mohammed al Fayed, no doubt said. Diana also revealed that she likes the Queen, and that deep down she still loves the Prince of Wales. Awwww.

Is it tacky to beam up the people's princess? (Might just get away with it on *Songs of Praise.*) Is it exploitative to resurrect a glamorous, golden goose in order to produce even more glittering eggs? Is the Pope a Catholic?

Nothing is too grotesque for the market to bear. In human – as opposed to show business – terms, it's understandable why grieving people want to contact the dead. Spiritualism took a quantum leap after the first world war, when vast numbers of young men were slain. Lots of charlatans have made a very healthy living out of the dead.

There are genuine "sensitives" out there as well, and there are many things in life and death we can't explain. The evidence, though, is that most of the "messages from beyond" are wincingly trivial. While it might be useful to learn in which hiding place granny's missing false teeth are to be found, it would be more humanly beneficial to be given the code for cancer, or even celestial intelligence about who will win the 2.30pm at Newmarket.

There is the question, too, of whether one would wish to be contacted in the great beyond. Churchill said he wanted to spend the first million years of eternity painting. Personally, I think it would be worth being deid just to get away from the mobile phone.

To prove that this undogmatic pay-per-view column is open to persuasion, though, I pointed the electronic croft's parapsychological dish towards heaven in order to see which glamorous celebrity might show up. Stand by for sensational revelations. (Simply send 50 euros, in used banknotes, to the electronic crofter, Orkney, then start reading.) Here is a transcript of the sacred event.

RF *(for it is me):* I am becoming aware of a ghostly presence....a tall, male figure is coming into view....he is wearing a crumpled suit, and his spectacles are slightly awry....Speak, sir, give this hungry freelance a world exclusive!

The ghostly figure: Um...hello, Ron....um...

RF: Donald! It's you! Donald Dewar! I can't believe it!

DD *(for it is he):* Yes, um, it's me.

RF: Are you enjoying yourself in heaven?

DD: Life isn't about enjoyment.

RF: But this is your afterlife! Surely you're entitled to a bit of fun after all your hard work on earth?

DD: Um, yes, um, I'm pursuing my enjoyable researches into 18th century Presbyterian divines. I'm speaking to them.

RF: That sounds great fun. Now tell me exclusively, Donald, what do you think about Jack McConnell?

DD *(changing into another crumpled suit):* Um....he is keeping up the standards set by Henry McLeish. That's the highest tribute I can pay him. Up here, I can see into the future, and I can tell you exclusively that the next First Minister will be a woman.

RF: Nicola Sturgeon! What a scoop!

DD *(wearing yet another crumpled suit):* Um...no....um....Wendy. Must go now. God has invited me for an audience, and there'll be food......

And that's it, folks. Now, I'm off to work on a fantastic idea for a television show. It'll be Big Brother, set in heaven. You'll be able to vote celebrities out of the Big Hoose in the sky. Will God be ejected before Diana? Watch this space. You can never accuse this righteous column of being tasteless, can you?

The Dirty Truth that Dare Not Speak its Name

The place we live in is a tip. By that I mean Britain. Having just travelled from Orkney in the north to London in the deep south – to visit my children, and the community of the Little Sisters of Jesus which I first encountered in Easterhouse – I can assert with confidence and shame that our country is a garbage-strewn dump.

The tragedy is that we have become used to it. We have grown up with rubbish. Only visitors see the offence, and most are too polite to point it out.

As I was leaving Orkney, the police and environmental health officers were launching a 'Clean up Orkney' campaign. Police were stopping litter louts and giving them a warning. Dog owners were being given scoops, and invited to clean up after their pooches.

It's not that Orkney is any dirtier than the rest of the country. Far from it. Its landscapes and seascapes are gorgeous, and the air quality is excellent. Yet litter, like the answer, my friend, is blowing in the wind. Some farmyards are repositories for rusting car and tractor wrecks.

"Bruck" is the expressive Orkney word for rubbish, and every April there is a "Bag the bruck" campaign. Community groups go off to the beaches armed with black plastic bags. They need lots of them. Those in peril or in pleasure on the sea throw overboard boxes, drums, poly bags, and other unmentionable objects. They treat the high seas as a skip. These treasures from the deep are disgorged upon our shores.

Why are we Brits such a grubby lot? Driving from Wick to Glasgow, I was treated to ghastly glimpses of bonnie Scotland. Garbage, garbage, everywhere. Cigarette packets, crisp bags, newspapers, fag-ends and bottles: these are the real emblems of visitscotland.com, the dirty truth that dare not speak its name.

Walking around Glasgow, I notice what I've always known: that the city of culture has turned itself into a film set for *The Wasteland.* If wading through beer cans, curry packs, cigarette packets and dogshit is what turns you on, then Glasgow's your dream place for a holiday. I enjoy Glasgow's boisterousness, but not its easy tolerance of garbage in a metropolis which boasts such magnificent buildings.

When we lived in Easterhouse, the broken windows and the omnipresent graffiti helped create an atmosphere of corporate despondency. On a family day-visit to St Andrews, our four-year-old daughter was amazed. "Where's the glass?" she asked, as she looked at the streets. She thought St Andrews was peculiar.

The trouble is that we human beings get used to anything. After a while, you don't notice graffiti and broken glass. It becomes background, especially if sheer survival is the name of your game. Yet its effect is insidious. The brutal environment forms a symbiotic relationship with the inner landscape of the spirit. Desensitisation is the result.

England is no better. Its green and pleasant land is another dump for detritus. As I make my way through parts of London, I pass gardens with old furniture lying in them. Skips overflow with plasterboard and ancient sofas. And people walk along the streets as if it were all normal.

That is the trouble: it is normal.

This pilgrimage through Britain has become a journey through junk. What is wrong with us? What is happening mirrors the way we abuse our precious planet. Middle Earth may be a creation of the fertile imagination of JRR Tolkein, but Midden Earth is the real-time creation of its ungrateful terrestrial inhabitants. It is humanity's terrible entry for the endgame global Turner prize.

While our fragile planet struggles for breath, along with our increasingly asthmatic children, the earth's non-renewable resources are burned up as if there were no tomorrow. We fight any proposal which threatens the right of the individual human adult to drive a motor car anywhere, any time.

Will our global leaders show us the way out of this mess? No. President George W. Enron and prime minister Tony Mittal will not change this state of affairs. The love affair with big business is too deep and enduring for that. Business itself is too committed to short-term gain to make voluntary changes which will cause pain for shareholders.

The British tragedy is that at a time when Labour, with a second landslide mandate, could take a radical lead, we have a decent and able premier whose primary need is to be liked. Nay, darling, *loved*. Until Blair acknowledges his power and approval addictions and goes into rehab, bullets need have no fear of being bitten.

What is needed, though, is not just government action, but a whole new public mindset. The rubbish culture can be changed. It's not so long ago, for instance, that cinemas and restaurants were thick with tobacco smoke, whether people liked it or not. And think about car seat belts. It's now second nature to belt up.

So here's a start for bonnie, blighted Scotland. The Scottish Executive puts some serious money into a national clean-up. After an advertising campaign, the police announce that hefty on-the-spot fines will be imposed on litter offenders. Community service clean-up becomes a mandatory punishment for certain anti-social crimes.

In a few years, there will be no way back to Scotland the Dump. And *The Hens' March to the Midden* will at last cease to be Scotland's real national anthem.

Fear and Loathing in Lochgelly

P arading the body beautiful along the beaches of our noble land may have been a less than rewarding experience so far this year (unless, that is, you've been on holiday in continuously-sunny Orkney). Being virtually naked in a freezing storm may not be the ideal holiday break. Even in some faraway places the flesh parade has been rained upon.

It must have been extremely galling to have sweated in the gym all winter with a view to looking bronzed and fit on familiar or exotic beaches. According to reports, males have been every bit as anxious as females to look the part, so much so that a new, troublesome, condition is manifesting itself.

Called "muscle dysmorphia", it afflicts muscular men who believe, despite all the evidence, that they look underweight and underdeveloped. No matter the image of strength which is reflected back to them from the mirror, they are convinced that they are puny.

Researchers from McLean Hospital, Belmont, Massachusetts believe that the new condition is almost a reverse form of anorexia nervosa, where a stick-like young woman is convinced that she is overweight, even though the scales tell her the opposite.

"We think the underlying pathology of the two conditions may be the same," says Dr Harrison Pope, "since they are both disorders of body image. The preoccupations simply go in opposite directions."

This new male condition is not simply an American problem. Some of the research was conducted in the UK. Apparently there are men who give up social life – and even, in extreme cases, their job – in order to spend more time in the gym. Pumping iron becomes an addiction which takes over their lives.

Society has been well used to body images of beautiful, slim girls which reduce other young women to despair. Women who have had several pregnancies and are keen to reclaim their former statistics are intimidated by the omnipresent role models. No matter how hard they try, they can't meet the perfection represented by the glamorous images.

Now, apparently, it's the turn of males to descend into inconsolable gloom. They feel inadequate when they see pictures of young men with muscular arms and legs and washboard stomachs. So they turn up at gyms in numbers, seeking to bring their body shapes nearer to the approved versions.

All of this is not new, of course. I can remember, as a 16-year-old miniscule, skinny youth - weighing about six stones when I was soaking wet - being browbeaten by pictures of Charles Atlas. Remember him? In the adverts for his body-building course, he was sprouting muscles everywhere. The heading was, "Don't let anyone kick sand in your face again!"

Now, no one had ever kicked sand in my face before: not only because they wouldn't even have noticed me lying on the beach, thinking I was a jellyfish or something, but because there were no beaches in Cowdenbeath. Determined that the strong men wouldn't kick coal dust in my face, I enrolled in the course.

I did all the exercises in a desperate attempt to make

a formidable Scottish mountain out of a Cowdenbeath molehill. I even consumed a foul-tasting, expensive food supplement. I stretched and lifted and compressed, then I did it all again. I made positive affirmations and prayed and tried to look scary. Then I looked in the mirror, hoping to see an incredible hulk who would be capable of creating fear and loathing in Lochgelly.

What looked back at me was the same skinny wee guy without an ounce of muscle. I looked like an Oxfam picture of a starving orphan. If anything, I had lost weight, as well as money. I was a failure.

Then, a year later, I suddenly started growing. And growing. And eating. The food stores in Cowdenbeath ran out of supplies. I ate half a cow for breakfast. This is what made me the man I am. At 6 foot 1, and 12 stones, I don't take prisoners at Central Park. And that's only on the terracing.

No, this problem is not new, but the scale of it is. The title of a book produced by Dr Pope and his team, The Adonis Complex: The Secret Crisis of Male Body Obsession, says it all. (The mythical Adonis was half man, half god, flitting between Mount Olympus and planet earth while he flexed his powerful muscles and looked at his reflection in shop windows. The preening semi-divine twit eventually got his comeuppance when he was gored by a wild boar.)

The book points out how the modern gym has become a place of obsession for many people. The treadmill, the steppers, the rowing machines, the barbells and the leg machines are instruments of the new body consciousness. When Puritanism meets vanity, the combination can produce despair in self-obsessed people, and joy to wealthy owners of leisure clubs.

Both men and women alike wear the best of designer gear as they pursue impossible, sweaty dreams. As my pal

Rowan Williams – blessings upon his archiepiscopal heid - might have put it, the twin temples of gleaming shopping malls and state-of-the-art gymnasia are crammed with devotees. There are mirrors everywhere in these shrines built to honour another Greek god, Narcissus.

I am unaffected by these things, of course. Just don't try to kick sand in my face. Not unless you feel you have to, that is.

The Electronic Hero and the Steaming Dung

As I sit, tapping these words into a computer in rural Orkney, I am pleased to learn that I am one of a new, elite breed – the "electronic crofter". David Ross, the *Herald's* authoritative Highlands and Islands journalist, reported this week that between 200-300 people in the far north and west of Scotland are doing freelance work from home.

The figure is reckoned to be a disappointing one. Ten years ago, the old Highlands and Islands Development Board entered into a partnership with BT to deliver a £20m upgrade of communications in the north and west.

At that time, Sir Robert Cowan, the HIDB chairman, said it was the most significant improvement to the infrastructure of the region since General Wade built his roads and bridges in the eighteenth century. The improved telecommunications system meant that the speedy transfer of large amounts of data around Britain, and indeed the world, was possible. The electronic gates to the north and west were swinging open.

The new technology has been successful in creating 3300 new jobs in the remoter areas, but most of them are in offices in centres such as Thurso, Stornoway and Kirkwall. What has proved more difficult to crack has been the problem of persuading more people to work from home. The small number of electronic crofters is down to the fact, it seems, that big firms like to manage staff closely, and most people prefer to work with others. Tele-cottaging remains a choice of the few.

So, here I am in the Ferguson croft, that ground-breaking centre of white-hot technology, surrounded by coos and beautiful April scenery. I've always wanted to be part of an elite, pioneering cadre. It feels great to be an electronic hero, at the technological cutting-edge, while a pile of steaming dung, delivered by a kindly neighbouring farmer, sits outside, minding its own business.

Being an electronic crofter is, on the whole, pretty good. If you're going to suffer from repetitive strain injury, you might as well endure it while looking out to the hills of Hoy, rather from some city midden. And when your system crashes, you get to play with dung. (When I was but a lad in Cowdenbeath, I used to be sent out with a wheelbarrow to follow horses. This character-building stuff made me the man I am. Now the horseshit follows me. That's called progress.)

Composing sentences at a screen by an island coast is a pleasurable form of journalism. It's also a solitary kind of existence. I think of my early days in journalism in Edinburgh when we all pounded away at big Underwood typewriters. You needed to do weight-training just to move the carriage along. There was noise, camaraderie and drinking, as well as creative expenses writing. (Well, we all hankered to be fiction writers.) Now, newspaper offices are like the silent movies, with everyone engrossed in screens. And you even need receipts! They've taken away hacks' human rights.

Up here, beyond time and space, the computer is a magical instrument. I thought the new technology would make writing difficult, but it's wonderful. The computer actually assists the creative process, because you don't even need to start at the beginning. You can cut and paste. You can write as many wild words as you want, then edit the text down to size. The machine even counts the words for you. Then you press a button, and, hey presto, the words sing through space to Glasgow in a nano-second.

And here is another privilege for the electronic crofter. You can, from rural Orkney, annoy large parts of Scotland. Or from Harris. Take John Macleod. Whenever he gets bored, he launches another search-and-destroy missile about evolution straight from his electronic croft into the city centre. As if on cue, normally calm and urbane people start foaming at the mouth. Gotcha! Again! And again! Just when the blood pressure had gone back to normal!

I suspect that John, who has himself evolved from Homo Freekirkus into something even more Byzantine, actually knows less about the origin of species than I do about the innards of my computer. But even if you're on the wrong side of the debate, there's nothing quite so en-joyable as seeing those "tolerant" liberals fulminating death threats. The good thing about being so far away is that people can't get at you with their bare hands. By the time they've saved up the air fare, their anger has subsided.

More than £350 return from Glasgow to Kirkwall: that's what it'll cost you to strangle your electronic crofter. And it militates against people coming to live in the islands. Jack McConnell was here on Tuesday to open the new Kirkwall International airport. He made sympathetic noises about cross-subsidies.

Brendan Dick, BT Scotland's general manager, is quoted as saying, "The number of teleworkers in the Highlands and Islands will increase as technology enables them not just to work from home, but to work on the move."

Only if moving about is affordable. If Jack doesn't do something about it, he will find my tractor on his lawn. It will have my name on it. Ferguson.

Must go. Your daring electronic crofter in the orange boiler suit has a pressing "hands-on" engagement with some steaming dung. Unfortunately, it cannot be shifted electronically. As the old farmer said, you get manured to it.

The Black Doomsday Theatre of the Absurd

S ome of my best friends are jailbirds. Some of my best friends are clerics. And they're the same people. The dog-collared trouble-makers will acquaint themselves – or, in some cases, reacquaint themselves - with the inside of a nick on Monday, before making an appearance in front of a stern-faced, bewigged presence. Before I explain all this, I should say that, as a journalist, I have a fair bit of experience of courtrooms myself, but, thus far, on the right side of the law.

Courtrooms can be places of high drama, and of farce. It is told of Glasgow Police Court that one day a German was brought up from the cells and accused of urinating in a public place. His English was poor, and the baillie asked if anyone in the court could speak German. One wee Glasgow man stood up. He was invited by the bench to ask the accused to confirm his name. There was a dramatic pause before the interpreter asked the bewildered man in the dock, "Vot is your name?" The Glaswegian had watched one war movie too many. This story surely has to be apocryphal, but stranger things have happened in the law courts of our noble land.

But what of my clerical friends? Why will they find themselves arraigned before a sheriff? They will have been charged with breach of the peace for lying in the road opposite Faslane nuclear base on the Clyde.

Now lying on a public road is not the healthiest way to pass a freezing February morning. But these normally law-abiding men and women of the cloth believe passionately that what lurks in the murky waters of the Clyde is not good for the health of humanity. They also believe that by averting our eyes from the horror on our doorstep, we are in serious danger of sleepwalking into a catastrophic nuclear war.

Before they move toward the Faslane gates to begin their non-violent protest, they will break bread and share wine. They will consciously bring to mind that historic, cruciform sacrifice at Golgotha, the place of the skull, and will make a link, trembling, with the contemporary hellish transfiguration of matter and nuclear energy which is "brighter than a thousand suns". The body of Christ, broken for you.

Awareness of the nuclear menace has receded in recent years. The ending of the Cold War has brought the impression of security. So the issue has gone on to the back burner. But the doomsday clock is still ticking quietly.

The Clyde is host to **HMS Vanguard, HMS Victorious, HMS Vigilant** and **HMS Vengeance,** nuclear submarines armed with 48 warheads. The total yield is equivalent to over 1000 Hiroshima bombs.

Trident is a first-strike weapon capable of destroying most of the Northern hemisphere in ten minutes. 30 million men, women and children would be wiped out in that time. The effects of radiation would make much of the earth inhabitable. The result would be what scientists call, chillingly, "nuclear winter".

Nuclear weapons are an accident or a military mistake waiting to happen. The notion of stability is illusory. The USA's plans for "Son of Star Wars" will up the nuclear ante and fuel a new stage in the arms race. We are living in a tinderbox which could reduce planet earth to an environment which cannot sustain human life.

In 1996, the International Court of Justice declared that it is illegal to use weapons which make no distinction between civilians and the military. The threat to use Trident, with its massive, indiscriminate overkill, seriously undermines our moral posturing before the developing world.

The cost of Trident is stratospheric. It has cost the equivalent of £30,000 a day since the birth of Christ. It has repeatedly been allowed to overspend by billions without penalty. Yet woe betide a local authority which goes over its budget by hiring some more home helps. The costs of implementing free care for the elderly are scrutinised minutely, yet Trident, apparently, can name its price. We are paying that price in so many ways; our very defence system is helping to create the conditions for the next war.

The clerics who will be lying on the road at Faslane during Monday's "Big Blockade" do not imagine that they are saving the world. Some of them will receive real hostility for their actions.

"Vot is your name?" asks the comic interpreter in the global, black, Doomsday theatre of the absurd. Our name is Adam. Our name is Eve. If we sleepwalk down the path to a wintry, cosmic Golgotha, our names, and the names of our children, will disappear from the face of the earth. We are living as if there were no tomorrow; and we may be right.

Do Not Answer Mobile Phone While Having Smear Test

Some people like a bit of rough from their doctor. Not for them the soothing bedside manner of the gentleman GP. They want a medic who goes straight for the jugular, and who tells them, in fairly brutal terms, what needs to be done. They thrill to a doctor who takes no prisoners, and who issues stern, even angry, lectures. It takes all kinds to make a ward.

Such a doctor presided over my own birth. He told my mother that I was the ugliest baby he had ever seen. Not just one of the ugliest. The ugliest baby in Cowdenbeath! Even uglier than Denis Canavan! By any known standards, that was an inauspicious start to life.

Next, the doc said to my mother, pointing at me: "Know what I'd do with him?" He then pulled his hand down on an imaginary toilet chain. Welcome to the world. He was joking. Wasn't he? It's the way he tells them. The story became a family legend, gleefully told to distant relatives and strangers, who would approach me pulling imaginary chains. And you think you've got problems.

Another general practitioner in my youth, Dr Falczynski, was a renowned terror. He was blunt to the point of rudeness. Yet his patients swore by him. He would lacerate them (verbally), and they would emerge from the surgery reeling, but radiant. Orgasmic, even. It might have been like being mugged by an ultra-presbyterian Jehovah on a bad hair day, but his thrilled devotees would say, breathlessly, "He's a great doctor, though." Those who survived the encounter got better, some miraculously. Healing is about more than pills.

All of this flashed through my mind when I read the results of a *Readers Digest* survey of GPs which showed that most would like to be able to be more blunt with their patients. It seems that they feel constrained, inhibited even, in the surgery. I can understand that. Nowadays, Dr Falczysnki, despite his track record of cures, would be sued for millions.

The survey revealed that up to half of all doctors today wish they could make personal observations, for example about patients' weight or standard of hygiene, while 60 per cent would like to be able to tell patients they do not need a prescription.

What might it be like if doctors' fantasies came true? Fortunately, this investigative column can tell you. Thanks to its much feared fly-on-the-wall technology, here are exclusive excerpts from a transcript from a day in a surgery at the western end of the Central Belt.....

Dr Blunt: "Come in, come in, it's fine tae see ye. How's yersel, yer looking grand?"

Fat Boab: "Ah'm feelin a bit sluggish efter the New Year, doactor. Can ye help me?"

Dr Blunt: "No, but you can help yourself, you obese layabout. You stuff yourself with food and drink, and you complain about feeling sluggish! It's because you're a slug! And why don't you get your hairy arse off your couch now and again, and move one leg in front of the other? Don't waste my time, you ignorant oaf!"

Fat Boab: "My, yer a great doactor! Ah feel better already."

Dr Blunt: "So do I. Next please!"

Duff Walker: "Doactor, Ah've got sair feet. Ah think they might need tae be amputated."

Dr Blunt: "Or even washed. Take off your shoes, for this is holy ground. My, these are holey socks. Good grief, Mr Walker, the stench is unbearable. I think I need a doctor. Out! Out! brief candle!"

Mrs McFlannel: "Dr Blunt, I've got an embarrassing wee problem. It's at the southern end of my hemisphere."

Dr Blunt: "You mean your bum."

Mrs McFlannel: "If you put it like that, yes. I think I'm suffering from haemorrhoids."

Dr Blunt: "You've got piles! This is your anus horribilis! Ha, ha, ha, ha, ha, ha....."

And so, reluctantly, we leave Dr Blunt, in the midst of another hard day at the orifices.

It's understandable that doctors feel frustrated. They get blamed for all the ills of the National Health Service; they get stood up by patients who fail to cancel appointments, they are deceived by punters who conceal the fact that they haven't been taking the prescribed medicines, they are berated because they don't hand out prescriptions. And there are those feet, which smell like they did walk in ancient times.

"What would I like to say to my patients? 'You smell'," stated one GP bluntly. Astonishingly, 50 per cent of doctors agree. What are the other things GPs would like to say to patients? Here are a few from the survey:

"Please do not answer your mobile phone while I'm doing your smear test."

"There's nothing really wrong with you – you need a social worker, not a doctor."

"No, you can't have a sick note when I'm feeling just as ill as you are."

"Please just answer my question!"

So this is what your respectable-looking doctor may really be thinking. Remember, you read it first in *The Herald*.

While the comforting bedside manner may have its uses, my hunch is that if we allowed our GPs to be a bit more honest – though a bit less direct than Dr Blunt – we might all be in rude health.

The Sugar Daddy in the Sky

God, said Albert Einstein, does not play dice. It seems, though, that He plays tennis. According to Goran Ivanisevic, who won the enthralling men's final at Wimbledon on Monday, God did the business for him on the day. Even before the final, God had moved in His mysterious ways by sending the rain which twice interrupted Goran's semi-final match with Tim Henman.

"God gave me rain on Friday," the unequivocal Croat explained, "and it saved me." Not only that, when play resumed, the Lord, apparently, more or less beat Henman for him. "I thank God because it is due to Him that I am in this final."

The supreme ruler of the universe also dealt with the problem of the stiffness in His servant's shoulder, and followed that by obligingly serving the ace which won the final – or at least nerved the sinews that made the winning serve. What was a little disconcerting was the sight of Ivanisevic sinking to his knees and crossing himself when his opponent put the ball out of court. Presumably what appeared to be an unforced error had actually been, well, forced by a higher hand.

Advantage, God.

After four failures in the Wimbledon finals, Goran was entitled to his victory. He is an engaging character who is difficult to dislike: a cross between a charismatic idealist and charming conman who knows how to wow his public.

One suspects that there is a bit more daylight between himself and his public theology than he cares to admit. One hopes there is. The notion of God sitting watching Wimbledon and ordering angels to massage Goran's shoulder, cause his opponent to double-fault, or send a rainstorm is endearing in a Walt Disney kind of way – unless, that is, your name happens to be Tim Henman or Pat Rafter.

The fantasy world of sport seems to breed this kind of schmaltzy religion. It is at its toe-curling worst on the American golf circuit, where God is repeatedly credited with holing putts on the eighteenth green. Billy Graham, who is often associated with this sort of stuff, was actually more down to earth out on the course with Presidents. "Prayer never seems to work for me on the golf course," he said. "I think it has something to do with my being a terrible putter."

Some years back, Brian Irvine, the devout Aberdeen captain, had to take the penalty kick which would win his side the Scottish Cup. As Pat Bonnar, the Celtic goalkeeper crossed himself, Irvine prayed – then scored. Did that make God a Protestant? Or simply an Aberdeen supporter? (If so, where is He now that they need Him?)

It was 'the hand of God' that defeated England, claimed Maradona, after he illegally palmed the ball into the net for the decisive goal. One of the best examples of the crossover between religion and sport is that of the fastest–ever recorded goal, scored by the Brazilian forward Ravolino.

Apparently, he had been tipped off that the opposing goalkeeper always said a prayer at the kick off. When the whistle blew, Ravolino whacked the ball straight at the goal. Three seconds later the goalkeeper opened his eyes to find that the ball was in his net. Bloody hell! The poor sod had been praying for a shut-out! Who says God doesn't have a sense of humour?

You don't have to be a sophisticated theologian to see that there are inherent problems in the notion of a supreme being who sends a rain shower to help Goran Ivanisevic defeat Tim Henman, but allows millions of people to die because of drought. As the graffiti puts it: "God is not dead. He is simply engaged on a less ambitious project."

The problem at the heart of all this is the concept of a divine idol who is simply a larger-than-life man, a superhuman person who can be charmed or manipulated, a sugar daddy in the sky. This is a diminished god who rewards favourites and graciously grants prosperity to those who pay their religious dues. It's a theology that works in a tongue-in-cheek way on the tennis court, but breaks down in the cancer wards. A sustainable contemporary religious belief has to get beyond the Sunday School.

The thinking which Goran crudely and rumbustiously represents extends way outside the confines of conventional religion. It has many secularised varieties. Triumphantly grinning Goran appeals to us because we often yearn for childhood certainties and visible signs.

As Woody Allen puts it: "I am plagued with doubts. What if everything is an illusion and nothing exists? In that case I definitely overpaid for the carpet. If only God would give me some clear sign: like making a large deposit in my name in a Swiss bank."

Randy Mr Bull Meets Miss Daisy

A Bible college in the Midwest of America used to advertise itself as "situated 20 miles from any known form of sin." Well, deep in the countryside, your worthy columnist is surrounded by ongoing sexual orgies. Far from being 20 miles away from sin, the electronic croft is set in the midst of shameless couplings which happen only a few feet away. Oh dear, oh dear.

Yes, the hills are alive not just with the sound of music, but with the sights of nature taking its course. Let me explain it for those of you who live in towns. Ms Daisy is chewing contentedly, when along comes showboating Mr Bull, formidable tackle swinging, master of all he surveys. After the minimum of chatting up, a panting Mr Bull is suddenly engaged in Mr Darwin's business.

And what does Ms Daisy do while several tons of sweaty geezer are on her back? She carries on munching the grass, thus confirming all these surveys showing that females prefer eating and shopping to sex. Mr Bull, having contributed yet again to a new generation, then lies down for a wee rest. Until, that is, he spots this shapely young cow with lovely legs. Dirty work, mutters Mr Bull, but somebody's got to do it.

Now this all seems distinctly unPresbyterian to me, but there it is. It's the way the Lord has ordained it. It's also the way, give or take a few adjustments, the Lord has ordained the continuation of the human species. While Presbyterians might have preferred it if the omnipotent Lord had chosen more seemly ways of arranging the pro-creation business, we just have to bare it and grin.

The biological drive in humans kicks in fairly early. The problem is that this isn't terribly convenient. A 14-year-old Master Bull inseminating a few hundred 13-year-old Miss Daisies is not particularly good for society. So what should be done about it?

One answer emerged this week. Schools in England and Wales are being invited to distribute condoms and birth control pills to pupils. The charity Parentline Plus, with the support of HM government, has advised parents to leave condoms casually around the house, so that their children may pick them up. The thinking is quite simple: "Young people are going to engage in sex. We want to cut down the number of unwanted babies. Free contraceptives, made available at school and at home, are what the situation requires."

This mindset needs to be examined carefully before it is accepted as received wisdom. What if the continual visibility of birth control devices, all with the imprimatur of adult authority, is an incitement to under-age sex?

Condoms given out at school – or strewn casually around the living room like a Turner prize-winning scene – send out a pretty clear message: "Have sex. It will be OK if you use one of these."

Despite the fairly easy availability of contraception for years, Britain has the highest rate of teenage pregnancy in Europe. One in three girls under 16 is sexually active. The dramatic rise in under-age sex has been accompanied by a huge increase in venereal disease. In the past five years, the incidence of sexually transmitted diseases has increased by more than 35% in Scotland. Doctors are so concerned that they are calling for a national screening programme.

These physical health issues are compounded by the psychological damage caused by too early exposure to sex. Apart from the distress originated by unwanted pregnancies among young people ill-equipped to deal with a baby, the emotional consequences of pre-mature sexual activity can be devastating.

I feel sympathy for health workers who are trying their best to deal with an acute social problem. Undoubtedly, if young people are going to be sexually active, it is preferable that they engage in safer sex. There is a problem, though, with a strategy which concentrates on the free distribution of condoms: it doesn't work; or, at least, it has very limited success. Yet its advocates think that the self-evident answer is to pursue the same one-track policy to destruction.

There is no apparent end to this road. Are contraceptive machines to be installed in primary schools? If not, why not? When will Primary 4 classes be engaged in putting condoms on bananas? At what point do people say, "This is not working. There has to be another way."

The problem is that this other way does not have quick-fix technological solutions. It requires a radical critique of the widespread sexualisation of our culture. The pressure on vulnerable young people is enormous. Sex has been elevated to a position of prime value, and those who question its pre-eminence are routinely demonised.

In Holland, where teenagers are five times less likely to become pregnant than their British counterparts, the safe-sex message is combined with discouragement of early sex. Issues of respect, commitment and choice are on the schools' agenda. In the USA, confidence-building courses intended to help teenagers deal with sexual issues are now being organised.

Going back to the so-called "good old days" of sexual repression is neither feasible nor desirable. Nevertheless, a counter-cultural revolution is required. It is impossible to parody the current obsession with sex. We are, it seems, a nation in heat.

Speaking of which, here comes Mr Randy Bull again. Ah, were it were so simple.

Time to Stand Up and Not be Counted

I would like you to raise a glass to Mr William Thornton, a brave politician notable for standing against the crowd. But before I extol the excellent virtues of a man whose name is not on everybody's lips, I must digress a little, and ask one or two questions.

Are you any good at counting? If so, you have a great future ahead of you in brave new 21st century Britain. Those who count the beans in our society are in the ascendancy, and will be for the foreseeable future. Who counts, wins.

The king sits in his counting house. So do Gordon Brown, the Count of Kirkcaldy, and Tony Blair, the Discount of Downing Street. They are counting not just our money, but hospital waiting lists, school exam passes, and everything that moves and breathes.

Counting is in. Counting has replaced politics.

The last general election campaign was so tedious because it largely consisted of cautious people in suits trading statistics. They were like school swots who had been up all night before the exam. What was astonishing was that vast numbers of percentage points on every possible topic were stored in these small but perfectly formed political heads. A question by an interviewer would trigger an avalanche of mind-numbing statistics.

Hugh Gaitskell was once famously described by Aneurin Bevan as "a desiccated calculating machine". So are they all, all desiccated calculating machines, spewing forth endless numbers until you are begging for mercy. This is the political nightmare: clones with speaking-clock voices, on message, regurgitating statistical answers to questions you haven't even asked. These litanies are delivered in passionless voices, even though words like "I passionately believe" are routinely tossed in every five minutes. We are deep into George Orwell country.

What is this obsession with counting and targets all about? It's partly because the main political parties are striving to occupy the same centre ground. The debate, therefore, is not so much about ideology as about statistics. But this quest for so-called 'objectivity' masks an ideology which is far from neutral. What it says, roughly, is this: you can monitor progress by measuring. If waiting lists are reduced, the health of the nation must have increased. If your school has a reasonable place in some 'league' table, you can be satisfied.

These are fallacies. Lies, damned lies, and statistics. By making hospital waiting lists its benchmark, the government can bodyswerve the crucial question of the quality of patient care. Because quality is not measurable, it literally doesn't count. School league tables do not tell us about the situation of housing scheme or rural schools. To pour everything through the number-crunching filter is to skew reality. Quality – and that is what really counts – cannot be measured in this reductionist way.

In the meantime, people are being driven to distraction by endless paperwork. Doctors cannot doctor because they're filling up forms. Teachers cannot teach because they are forever doing statistics or photocopying reports. The new ideology does not favour quality – it favours those who can work the system. It also promotes malign rule by bureaucrats. This is not progress. In short, politics by numbers offers a fraudulent prospective.

One of the people who has done most thinking about this is David Boyle, author of *The Tyranny of Numbers*. He points out that measurement as obsessively practised by our society is all about standardisation and control. We will have children who can pass exams, he says, but have no judgment. We will have doctors who translate our symptoms into numbers before feeding them into the computer. We will be turning ourselves ever so slowly into machines.

When politicians and civil servants finish counting waiting lists and exam lists, they start counting the punters. We've just had another census: which brings me neatly back to Mr William Thornton. He was a Yorkshire Member of Parliament in the eighteenth century. When a bill to introduce the first-ever census was brought before parliament in 1753, William Thornton was the only MP to vote against the measure. He argued that national counting would be followed by the introduction of some fairly pernicious institutions. He whipped up such strong opposition in the country that when the matter came to the House of Lords, the bill was thrown out.

Mr Thornton was a far-seeing man, even though he knew it was only a matter of time before his arguments would be overruled. He could see that the tyrannical state would be founded upon mediocrity and statistics. He was right. If you look at life statistically, you end up like Michael Portillo of blessed memory – may his quiff rest in peace – exulting in the poll tax.

Can the trends be reversed? It is still not too late to stand up and not be counted.

Apocalypse Right Now

AND WHEN he had opened the fourth seal, I heard a voice of the fourth beast say, "Come and see". And I looked, and behold a pale horse: and his name that sat on him was Death, and Hell followed with him. And power was given unto them over the fourth part of the earth, to kill with sword, and with hunger, and with death, and with the beasts of the earth. Book of Revelation, chapter 6.

On Tuesday, September 11, at 13.50 GMT in the year of Our Lord 2001 – which, by any normal method of counting, is the year of the millennium – the silly season was formally declared closed. It was replaced by the season of the Apocalypse, the dread season of the four terrible horsemen, the ferocious season of trembling and fearfulness.

Oh, sinner man, whereya gonna run to, all on that day? The desperate scenes of terrified people fleeing from the melting, dissolving towers of the World Trade Centre in New York, smoke cascading down in white waterfalls, had an eerie, biblical, filmic quality. *Apocalypse Right Now.* And all at a television set near you.

The shocking images of a direct assault on the greatest military and financial power in the world will stay in the brain forever. The American psyche has been damaged, certainly for the lifetime of its children who watched the American Dream melt into the American nightmare.

How will the United States of America interpret its own Doomsday Event? America has the highest level of church-going in the world. A high proportion of the population describe themselves as born-again believers, and within that mix of literalistic religion, high consumerism and social conservatism, apocalyptic thinking is very strong: as it is, of course, in Islamic fundamentalism.

Apocalyptic literature is the kind of writing which deals with the 'end times'. It tends to flourish at times of great insecurity, or persecution. The most famous apocalyptic text of all is the Book of Revelation, with its spooky talk of the four Horsemen of the Apocalypse, a great Endtime battle between the forces of good and evil at Armageddon in Israel, a 1000-reign of Christ, and a 'rapture' when the elect are taken up into heaven.

The Book of Revelation was originally an underground document, designed to stiffen the resistance of Christians under persecution by the Roman emperor. With its secret codes and symbols – all designed for its own times – it is notoriously difficult to interpret. For that very reason, it is a happy hunting ground for starey-eyed maniacs, some of them very dangerous indeed. Take some of the numbers in the book, multiply them then throw them in the air and, hey presto, you've got the date of the Second Coming.

Endgame thinking crosses over many religions: witness the Waco and Davidian massacres, the Order of the Solar Temple, and the Japanese Aum Shinrikyo sect. But fascination with epochs and seasons is by no means just a religious fixation. Marxism and Nazism showed similar obsessions in their brands of secular millenarianism.

It is particularly dangerous when politicians see themselves as actors in an apocalyptic drama. Ronald

Reagan self-confessedly viewed himself through this distorting looking glass, and it affected his policies towards Israel. When he denounced Russia as "an evil empire" he was playing the apocalyptic game; so is Islam when it denounces America as 'the great Satan'.

This is combustible stuff, and the stakes are very high. When barbarism is combined with high-tech skills and a willingness to die for a cause – and the devastating consequences are transmitted live across the face of the globe – a new insecurity is let loose in the world. We all seek understanding and reassurance. Yet the apocalyptic insistence that God is arranging all this, like a master puppeteer in the sky, is to remove the issue from its proper locus – that of human responsibility.

Here is an alternative theological approach: the biblical notion that the sins of the fathers may be visited on future generations. America has drawn such hatred to itself not because of its biblical righteousness but because of its domineering and arrogant approach to much of the rest of the world. Whether it be Third Word debt, the burning up of fossil fuels as if there were no tomorrow, global warming, trading arrangements with poorer nations, or Son of Star Wars, America's lack of humility and sometimes even humanity makes it increasingly vulnerable to attack. Yet America should not stand in the dock alone.

This week's atrocity will add to the catastrophic strain which already runs through much of our contemporary thinking, religious or otherwise. Below the surface can be detected deep strains of pessimism and, even worse, fatalism.

Our biggest danger lies not in external catastrophes, real or imagined, but in our sense of impotence. If it's not gods, it's politicians, and we cannot influence any of them. The die is cast. We are merely bit players in the deterministic cosmic drama.

The transformation that is required is not about finding cleverer technical solutions to difficult problems, but about reconnecting with each other. Here is an even more fruitful theological avenue to explore: our truly human vocation is to see our neighbour – in the street and at the other end of the world – as a bearer of sacredness. In these troubling, difficult times, this is the only wisdom left to us.

No more houghmagandie on the lawn, please

So it's no more sex in the garden, then. Giving that up is going to be pretty hard. Nothing like a bit of houghmagandie on the front lawn while the neighbours are watching, but there it is. The government is determined to put a stop to it in the name of public decency.

The cry of "Come into the garden, Maude," must cease forthwith. Only plants will be allowed to do it, providing they've got a government permit.

In explanatory notes published with the new Sexual Offences Bill, the Home Office said an offence would be committed if a sex act took place in a private place and "where activity in that place can be seen in a public place". The notes said: "An example would be a private garden which can be seen from the street." The proposals will in some cases apply in Scotland under UK law and in other cases will be piloted by the Scottish Executive.

People who engage in sexual congress in the back garden will face jail sentences of up to six months. Six months in Barlinnie for a spot of aerobic gardening! Jings, mass murderers get less. Everything in the garden might be lovely, but the aftermath could be a bit excruciating.

The jail sentences apply only to humans. Hedgehogs,

dogs, birds and midges which are caught with their breeks about their ankles will be given community service. It'll be a "three strikes and you're out" job. A second offence, and the creatures will be tagged electronically. In court for a third time, it'll be off to Robben Island for life. Got to put a stop to the outbreaks of sex in gardens which is disfiguring our national life. It's quite likely that even the gnomes are at it as soon as your back is turned. Not very Presbyterian conduct, really.

I hadn't realized that garden sex was such a national sport. Like the sixties, I must have missed it. I've heard of *Sex in the City,* but not *Sex in the Garden.* All these gardening programmes on TV have probably been full of double entendres, and I didn't even realize it. All that chat about tools and bedding plants is now seen in a new light.

Actually, engaging in such behaviour in Orkney in February might lead to prison, but only by way of intensive care. You'd be on a life support machine for weeks. The winter weather has been such that even the legendary brass monkeys would be taking a reality check. "Your tiny hand is frozen" might not be the only song in town.

Now here is the greatest irony of all: if it weren't for sex in the garden, we wouldn't be here at all. What do I mean? The Garden of Eden is what I mean. The ageless story says that Adam and Eve set the human ball rolling. We know the official version, but here is the unauthorised version, vouchsafed to me personally by a speaking snake.

"While Adam and Eve were together, a keeper of the law, a policeman, saw them, and saith unto them: "Oi, oi, then, wot's goin' on 'ere?" And Adam spake unto the keeper of the law: 'We are being fruitful and multiplying.'

'You can't do that 'ere,' saith the keeper of the law. 'This is a bleedin' garden, mate. You can get six months in the nick for this. The neighbours might see you.' Adam saith unto the keeper of the law, 'There are no neighbours. How did you get 'ere, I mean here, by the way?' The keeper of the law replied, 'I came on my motorbike.'

'No,' saith Adam, 'I mean how did you come to exist?' The keeper of the law looked up to the heavens and replied, 'It's a bleedin' mystery, mate. Anyway, I'll let you off with a warnin' this time, but any more of this procreatin' in a garden and you'll be banged up.'

'Cor blimey,' saith a snake, as it slithered by."

So, there it is. Ever since then, gardens have been the location of choice. Ernest Simpson, the second husband of Mrs Wallis Simpson – who, who we now know got up to no good with Guy Trundle, an improbably-named car salesman – was described by Lady Diana Cooper as "an awful, common little man, the sort of creature who was always trying to get you into the garden." No wonder gardens are now out of bounds.

There's good news among the gloom, though. According to the government, consenting adults will be allowed to have sex at home with the curtains open. Whoopee! I was worried in case I'd have to give that up. We do that in Orkney all the time – even sell tickets for such events, especially during the tourist season.

The Bill said a distinction was drawn if sex took place inside a "dwelling". It said: "Where A has sex in his bedroom, leaving his curtains open so he knows there is a risk he will be seen from the house opposite, he does not commit an offence." In other words, if you're thinking about sex in the garden, forget it. But if you want to do it in your floodlit window, that's fine. There is something glorious about civil servants drafting legislation on sex offences. You couldn't make this stuff up.

There's more. You can have sex in a public toilet as long as you – wait for it – close the cubicle door. In for a penny, in for a pound. The wondrously-named Home Office minister, Mr Hilary Benn, who outlined the Bill, said: "If the cubicle door is open, then clearly an offence is committed. If it's closed it is different." This is presumably known as "doing it at your convenience".

You know the craziness about all this? There's a box in everyone's living room which shows wall-to-wall fake sex night and day. These shows are made by exhibitionists for the nation of jaded voyeurs we have become. Isn't there a great deal of hypocrisy in this new Sex Act?

Following a Trail of Conscience

The distinguished man sitting beside me at table in the electronic croft is philosophical. He knows that what he is doing is not going to change the world, yet he still believes he has to do what he is doing. At the age of 74, and after major surgery for prostate cancer, he is following a trail of conscience.

Former Roman Catholic priest Bruce Kent rose to prominence in the 1950s and 1960s as a radical leader of the Campaign for Nuclear Disarmament. At a time when big CND marches stopped the traffic in London, Monsignor Kent's passionate advocacy of a worldwide campaign to stop the spread of nuclear weapons, starting with Britain, gained him many admirers and critics.

The more prominent he became, the more enemies he attracted. Letters were sent to the Vatican, calling for his dismissal from holy orders. How dare a Christian priest go on television to suggest that an ostensibly Christian nation try to break the spiralling build-up of weapons of mass destruction by unilaterally taking a step back! Among those who agreed with him were young politicians such as Tony Blair, Gordon Brown and Robin Cook.

By the early 1980s, the pressure on Cardinal Hume to sack him was intense, but the Cardinal supported him. The embattled Monsignor Kent eventually decided to walk, not only for his own health's sake, but for the sake of his superiors. The vocational decision to concentrate his energies on peacemaking in the world instead of defending himself in ecclesiastical rows was a costly one. He remains a practising Catholic, but misses the priesthood.

As well as being vice president of CND, he is also leader of the Movement for the Abolition of War. How can anyone with eyes to see and ears to hear believe in the abolition of war? Surely this is naïve beyond belief, risible even? Bruce Kent's basic point is simple: with the nuclear firepower now available, humanity is looking at the end of history unless it finds alternative means of resolving disputes. Simplistic? Of course. Against common sense? Yes. But in the increasingly apocalyptic world we inhabit, we need the saving knowledge of uncommon sense.

We rise from the dinner table. For the man who was once regularly in the living rooms of the nation via the television screen, the city and royal burgh of Kirkwall is now calling. On the drive in from the country, I worry as to whether anyone will turn up. After all, very few people nowadays show up for public meetings. Even such a popular figure as local MSP Jim Wallace, Deputy First Minister for Scotland, would struggle to fill a hall.

I needn't have worried. Extra chairs have to be brought into the main hall of the new St Magnus Centre. There is a real buzz. Bruce Kent is listened to intently by men, women and young people who are concerned about the impending war with Iraq.

Kent eschews histrionics, but he is a fine platform speaker. He talks about the street in which he lives in North London. It has many nationalities. Yet people do not resolve disputes by shooting each other. Why not? Because, says the speaker, no one lies in the gutters dying of starvation. There is an elected council. There is a police force. There are recognised courts of law.

58

In the real world of dangerous international disputes, many people starve to death. Trade rules support the powerful. International courts are not honoured. United Nations resolutions are supported by the big powers only when it suits their purposes. Kent argues that if there is no respect for international law and global human rights, then nuclear armageddon awaits.

On this wintry night in Kirkwall, Bruce Kent is alive, vibrant, as he engages with the audience. As I look around the hall, dedicated to Orkney's Viking peacemaker saint, I remind myself of the weaponry which is available. The UK alone spends £4m a day on nuclear weapons. The current British nuclear arsenal is equal to the power of 1500 Hiroshimas, enough to slay not just millions of innocents, but the earth itself.

Whatever opportunities there were in the 1960s for Britain to take a lead in the disarmament process are now long gone. Even the peace dividend following the fall of the Berlin wall has largely been squandered. And now we prepare for war again. A pre-emptive strike will happen, whether United Nations agrees or not.

Back at the electronic croft, we enjoy a glass of Orkney's Highland Park. It is clear that this man will travel and speak about alternatives to war as long as he has breath in his body. After all these years, his idealism and enthusiasm are undiminished. Before he goes to bed, he phones his wife, Valerie, to tell her of his day. Whether he will see the peace he desires is highly unlikely; but he is clearly at peace with himself. I am glad of the presence of this good man, glad to have him in my home.

It's the Ratings, Stupid

BBC Radio Scotland's decision to drop its 15 minute Friday morning slot *Man Bites Dog* is a straw in a contemporary wind which blows increasingly chill. Presenter Tom Morton is a witty, acerbic, razor-sharp, entertaining journalist, whose programmes are never dull. He's been elbowed aside to make way for Fred MacAulay, who already broadcasts from Monday to Thursday.

Now, I have nothing against Mr MacAulay. In fact, it is very hard to have anything against Mr MacAulay. He is amiable, pleasant, and sometimes amusing. What is truly tiresome about his show, though, is the fact that he has studio guests whose function in life is to laugh hysterically whenever the great man utters anything which is deemed to be remotely funny. Anyone who is interviewed is continually subjected to Mr Macaulay's puns and asides (cue more manic braying.) In short – is it permissible to say this? – Fred MacAulay for Tom Morton is a poor exchange.

The substitution is part of a BBC philosophy which decrees that any broadcaster who gets good ratings must be given more and more air time. Hence, Fred MacAulay is everywhere. (At least, it feels like it. George MacLeod used to ask the question: why do Presbyterian ministers speak longer than other people? Answer: they don't, it just feels like it.)

To give Fred his due, he broadcasts like a man who can't believe his luck every morning, and will enjoy it until he's been found out. (And who designed the toe-curlingly arch trailers for the Friday morning extension? "All the Fred you want. Fred: now giving it to you five days a week – and loving it!" Yes, yes, we get it. Now please stop treating us all like morons.)

Here are some more contemporary markers on the long march to civilisation.

Item 1. *This Morning* Quiz Show, hosted by Richard and Judy.

Richard: What nationality is the actor Anthony Hopkins?

Contestant: Er...

Richard: Look-you boyo...*(sings)* We'll keep a welcome in the hillsides...

Contestant: Scottish?

Richard: No! How green was my valley....

Contestant: Irish.

Item 2. The most recently published dictionary of quotations has ditched over 1000 citations from the Bible and Shakespeare.

Item 3. *This Morning* Quiz Show, hosted by John Leslie.

Leslie: On which street did Sherlock Holmes live?

Contestant: Er....

Leslie: He makes bread....

Contestant: Er.....

Leslie: He makes cakes....

Contestant: Kipling Street.

Item 4. An editorial in the *Scotsman* refers to Pontius Pilot. The Roman governor presumably trained with British Airways.

Item 5. BBC 2's *The Weakest Link* hosted by Sourpuss of the Year, Anne Robinson.

Robinson: Which product had an advertising ban

imposed on it in 1999?

Contestant: Marmalade.

Item 6. David Beckham, captain of England, talking about his son, Brooklyn: "I'd like to get him christened, but I'm not sure into which religion."

Item 7. *This Morning* Quiz Show, hosted by Richard and Judy.

Richard: What is the capital of Canada?

Contestant: Er....

Judy: It begins with "C".....

Contestant: Cowdenbeath?

Okay, I just made that last one up, but all the rest are true, recorded for posterity by *Private Eye* and *The Guardian*.

These random tidings from the ever-spreading realm of Dumbadoon hardly prove that we're a' doomed, but they are part of a trend. Take so-called 'reality tv'. This week, Mel Hill, one of the contestants in *Big Brother,* voiced her concern that she was manipulated by the producers of the voyeuristic show. A script written by the producers for her introductory video included the line: "I'm Mel, and I'm a sexy little babe."

"I feel angry with the programme-makers," said Hill, "because we had no idea what they were going to do with all the footage, and what they did with it was manipulate it into little stereotypes. I think the term 'reality tv' is totally misleading. It's not real. It is tabloid tv."

To voice these issues is inevitably to be charged with elitism and arrogance. The principal accusers are verbose Professors of Anal Retention who are running courses like "The Implications of Becks and Posh Iconography" at converted outside toilets masquerading as universities. Their arguments are the usual wearisome reruns of the old stuff about everything being relative, and nothing being inherently better than anything else. On this basis, excellence is an empty concept, Jeffrey Archer is as praise-worthy as Charles Dickens, Mystic Meg is as wise as Socrates, and Anthea Turner is as fascinating as Einstein. It's the ratings, stupid.

Here is the tragedy. We have countless television channels, all the resources of the internet, and instant digital communications across the world, yet we're drowning in an ever-expanding sea of mind-numbing drivel. Why does our expensive education system produce so many tv-conforming grunting catatonics who don't know their Shakespeare from their shampoo ads, and are seriously overdosing on junk-food for the mind?

What is even more sad is that the grubby levelling down is not seen as a tragedy, but as a liberating 'democratisation of culture'. This is a particularly vicious form of inverted snobbery which, for all its populist posturing, seriously patronises ordinary people. The language of mediocrity-posing-as-democratisation is, in reality, the language of cultural brain death.

When stupidity becomes the accepted norm, we are all losers. In the meantime, George W. Bush, potential global leader with a finger on the nuclear button, doesn't know the name of the President of Pakistan, and thinks that the inhabitants of Greece are called Grecians. Presumably Grecians 2000. Still, mustn't worry. We have all the Fred we want, giving it to us five days a week.

Jesus, Michelangelo and Lorenzo Amoruso

J ings! What a fright! When I got my *Herald* on Tuesday, there, staring at me from the front page, was none other than your actual Jesus. A starey-eyed Jesus. A lock-up-your-weans Jesus. Now, I know that the paper has had some good exclusives recently, but this surely topped the lot.

Urgent questions flooded my mind. Were the *Herald* photographic team really that old? Did Judas Iscariot have a Brownie box? Were the negatives found in an urn beside the Dead Sea? Had Max Clifford been involved?

When I read on, my hopes were dashed. It was only a computer-generated image made by the BBC for a new programme about Jesus. The photo-fit image was "based on detailed historical research". Presumably they found Mary and Joseph's family album.

Some years ago, while visiting a family in Easterhouse, a blockbuster film about Jesus was on the telly. The part of Christ was played by the actor Robert Powell, who was tall, handsome, fair-haired and blue-eyed. He looked like a GI in a toga, with a tea-towel on his heid.

"Robert Powell's just like Jesus!" exclaimed the swooning matriarch of the household. How did she know? Our ideas of Jesus's appearance are based on various artists' representations down through the centuries. Generally speaking, he has looked like an Italian; that's because most of the artists were Italian. Michelangelo, Rubens et al have had him looking uncannily like Lorenzo Amoruso of Rangers.

British Sunday School pictures have portrayed Jesus as white-skinned and fair-haired, usually carrying a foot-and-mouth-free lamb and looking like a right plonker. And, yes, the Hollywood movies invariably feature a square-jawed all-American guy. (And do I really recall Charlton Heston as a centurion drawling, "Surely this was the Son of Gaad", or was that a bad dream?)

It's all good, clean fun as long as you don't take it seriously. Sam Goldwyn Mayer said that he never lost money underestimating the public's taste. (Enter, on left, Sir Cliff slaughtering the Lord's Prayer to "Auld Lang Syne"). Look – as that other messianic figure would say – nobody has a scooby what Jesus looked like. The Gospel writers don't tell us. Strange though it may seem to an image-dominated generation, they simply weren't interested. Jesus might have looked like the hunchback of Notre Dame for all we know. He might have been ugly. He might have had an Arthur Scargill hairstyle, with the flying strands parted somewhere round about his right oxter. Does it matter? The glamourising stuff doesn't come from the Bible.

What we can say for sure about Jesus is that he was neither fair-haired nor white-skinned. He was a Palestinian Jew. (Jesus wasn't even a Christian. He started the whole Christian thing off, and maybe regrets it now, seeing some of the truly ghastly things that have been done in his name).

What the countless representations of Jesus down the centuries do is to capture some aspects of the man. Many of these images are called icons – pictures which are venerated because of their power to evoke devotion. I have in my study a 15th century Russian Orthodox icon of "Our Saviour the Wet Beard", showing a swarthy, dark, mysterious Christ. The original is in Nidaros Cathedral, Trondheim, the mother church of Orkney's St Magnus Cathedral. It is a very powerful picture.

When I was in India, I discovered, time and again, images of the fair-skinned, blonde, Jesus. These were portraits which had come via western missionaries, who thought they were handing over the "true" picture of Christ. It was part of the cultural imperialism which had natives wearing Y-fronts and singing "Jerusalem". Yet Jesus would have looked more like an Indian than the inoffensive English public school boy who was being foisted upon them. Before I left India, I was given a breathtaking portrayal of Jesus by an Indian artist; here was a dark-skinned Saviour with the pupil-less eye of ancient Indian art.

Powerful religious art can move to tears, and to worship. Part of the problem of understanding Jesus is that everyone brings their own cultural preconceptions to the task. Every 'Christian' culture co-opts him. The man who drove the moneylenders out of the temple is unashamedly presented as the Chamber of Commerce Man of the Year. The one who was executed as a disturber of the peace is portrayed variously as the *Sunday Post* Doc, Rev IM Jolly, basher of gays, and Daniel O'Connor.

Yet the fact that so many attempts have been, and are still being, made to portray Jesus indicate the enduring, yet elusive, power of the Nazarene. Even though he has been domesticated and sanitised by the Church, he cannot be contained, not even by death itself. His physical appearance is irrelevant; what truly gets under the skin is his profoundly disturbing, yet transfiguring, presence.

One Foot in Eden

Tomorrow night, they will gather at midnight for serious business. They will have hipflasks at the ready, thus ensuring that their night-time labours are convivial as well as competitive. Then the covers will come off the drivers, and play will begin in earnest. This is Orkney on the longest day of the year.

The 21st of June is an important day in the calendar of the northern isles for two reasons. We'll come to the second aspect later. Tomorrow in Kirkwall, assuming that there is not too much low cloud, people will read a copy of the local paper, *The Orcadian,* on their doorstep at midnight.

On Tuesday night, my wife and I had a meal with friends. At midnight, we were looking out over Stenness Loch, drinking an extremely potent liqueur made with boolace berries. Not quite Coleridge sipping green absinthe before writing *The Rhyme of the Ancient Mariner,* but it fair sets you up for a *Herald* column. Absinthe makes the heart grow fonder; Orcadian midnight's boolace makes the mind go yonder.

The seasons and the weather are important here, much more so than in Scotland's cities. Severe gales will mean that the ferries to Orkney will not run. Fog, which often follows a warm spell, rules out air travel. You will expect neither mail nor newspapers when that happens.

If you're going on holiday abroad, you need to allow an extra day or two to get from Orkney to the mainland airport from which your charter flight will leave. Going down the day before is no use. If there is fog, you can wave goodbye to your holiday.

Tomorrow, too, crowds of visitors will pour into Orkney for the beginning of the St Magnus Festival. This midsummer revel of music and drama draws visitors from all over the world. There is not a bed to be had in Kirkwall.

But now, the light in Orkney is luminous, magical. We've had the best spring and early summer for years. The rain in Spain – and in Glasgow and Edinburgh – may be falling mainly on the plain, but not here, not here. The farmers are crying out for moisture. Visitors to Orkney have been enchanted.

With its big skies, Orkney lets in the light in a way which leaves urban dwellers open-mouthed. The late evenings are gorgeous. The wind drops, and there is stillness. You walk the dog at midnight, and witness the glory of the pink. You enjoy every day, because you know that from now on the slow shift of the earth's axis will move Orkney inexorably towards darkening winter.

That's why these rituals of June 21 are so important. The golf at midnight and the reading of the newspaper are communal markers: a celebration of what is, set against an awareness of what is to come. The dark will arrive soon enough.

Orkney has known dark days in another sense, too. It was a cockpit of war twice last century. Scapa Flow was a major shelter for the British fleet in both world wars, and was the scene of the terrible sinking of **HMS Royal Oak,** with the loss of 833 men. It was because of the fateful intrusion of that treacherous German submarine that the Churchill Barriers were built, too late.

On June 21, 1919, two young girls, both of whom I got to know well in their latter years, were part of a school excursion on board the steamer, **The Flying Kestrel.** The plan was to get a close-up view of the German ships interned at Scapa Flow. Minnie Gorie and Peggy Gibson saw something which they were never to forget.

The Armistice expired on June 21. Vice-admiral von Reiter had no information from Germany, and the only British newspaper he saw, declaring that Germany had not accepted the peace terms, was four days out of date. He obeyed an old command not to allow German ships to fall into enemy hands; just after noon that day, he gave the order to scuttle the ships. One by one, the 72 ships sank slowly from view.

An artist who was painting the scene at Scapa was amazed to see his subjects disappear in front of him. The excited younger schoolchildren thought the show had been put on for them. But there was some firing, and nine German sailors were killed. The red stuff in the water was human blood.

On that bright Orcadian midsummer day, these schoolchildren from Stromness saw their innocent view of the world dissolve before their eyes. If sun-drenched Orkney was their garden of Eden, the Fall had entered in.

The Orkney poet Edwin Muir talks about the darkening moral landscape:

One foot in Eden still, I stand
And look across the other land.
The world's great day is growing late,
Yet strange these fields that we have planted
So long with crops of love and hate.
Time's handiworks by time are haunted,
And nothing now can separate
The corn and tares compactly grown.

The armorial weed in stillness bound
About the stalk; these are our own.
Evil and good stand thick around
In the fields of charity and sin
Where we shall lead our harvest in.

Light and dark. As with September 11th, you don't
know what you've lost until it is gone. Cherish the light
when it is here. Celebrate it.

Talking like Christ, Acting Like Caesar

Dear President Bush: Greetings from bonnie Scotland! I know that you are proud of your Scottish connections, so I thought I'd write you a wee note. You are on record as admiring Scottish quality, so I imagine that you read the *Herald* every day. Anyway, this will save me having to pay for a stamp – a notion which, I'm sure you'll know, appeals to the Scottish heart.

I'm writing this letter to you from the sacred island of Iona, where the rain is pouring down. Just as well it's the summer. You will be aware that Iona was one of the great European springboards for Christian mission, and nowadays it attracts pilgrims from all over the world, many from America. As a religious man yourself, you will understand what draws them to this historic spiritual site.

You have made no secret of your Christian belief: in fact, you have drawn attention to it on a number of occasions, particularly during your campaign for election. You said recently that Jesus Christ was your favourite philosopher, and the words 'God bless America' are rarely far from your lips.

In fact, this is what I want to talk to you about. Surrounded as I am by symbols of Christian faith, ancient and modern, I want to ask you, the most powerful man in

71

the world, how you relate your Christian belief to your political actions. Because I am confused.

Day by day, the reading of the runes points to the fact that you are planning to invade Iraq. Can I ask what Christian justification you have for your action? If Jesus Christ is your favourite philosopher, what exactly are the Christian philosophical principles which lie behind your intended action?

You say that it is wrong and dangerous for Iraq to possess nuclear weapons. I agree with that. Yet you make this argument as Christian president of the most heavily armed nuclear power the world has ever seen. Am I missing something here? How can you tell Iraq – and indeed Pakistan and India – that the possession and threatened use of nuclear arms is wrong, while your Christian index finger hovers over a button which can unleash Armageddon upon the world?

You will know that the Christian doctrine of the 'just war' permits a war of defence which is properly authorised and is fought under certain clearly defined conditions. You are about to launch a pre-emptive attack which is not, and will not be, supported by United Nations, and which will use utterly disproportionate firepower.

'Might is right' is not a doctrine which is to be found in the scriptures. Mr President, you are talking the language of Christ, while acting like a blood-stained Caesar. The fall-out – physical, economic, political, moral and spiritual – hardly bears thinking about. You talk about democracy in Iraq – where the CIA once funded Saddam Hussein, as well as supporting Osama bin Laden – while propping up authoritarian tyrants.

If September 11 has taught us anything, it is that in the high-tech global village we now inhabit, there are no hiding places. The erection of billion-dollar security systems – all at a time when Africa faces its own starvation

holocaust – cannot protect us. Right through the scriptures
there is an insistent drumbeat: God insists on justice for
the poor, and condemns illusions based on human hubris.
Brother George: what do you make of all this?

And what do you make of the saying of Jesus, your
favourite philosopher, commanding us to feed the hungry,
clothe the naked, visit the prisoner, and house the home-
less? Jesus says that whatever we do to the least of these,
we do to him; indeed, he says that ultimately we will be
judged by how we respond to human need. We are invited
to see our neighbour of whatever nationality or creed as a
person of dignity and worth created in the image of God.
Our neighbour, even our enemy, is us. Unless we work out
just ways of living in the global community we will perish
together.

None of this is to justify the evil of terrorism. But the
biblical witness is clear: any powerful empire which im-
poses unjust conditions upon the powerless and bankrupts
the poor comes under the judgement of God, either in
history or outwith history.

Mr President, you'll be thinking after all this that I'm
even blaming you for the weather. Well, come to think of
it....When Queen Street station is flooded at the beginning
of August, we are living in apocalyptic times. Queen Street
station! By the rivers of Glasgow we sat down and wept.

There is a direct connection between our profligate use
of the earth's resources and destructive climate change. Yet
you will not sign the international Kyoto protocols which
will protect diminishing fossil fuels and limit noxious emis-
sions. Which particular Christian reflections lead you to
that piece of non-action?

George, Christian brother, you'll be thinking
that all this is self-righteous. I plead guilty. But I also plead
with you to think through the implications of your faith,
and not dishonour it. It is little wonder that the 'Christian'

73

west – Britain is implicated in all this – is hated by so many people in the world.

The rain on Iona has stopped now. There are glimpses of sunshine, and a hint of a rainbow. God bless America. And God bless you.

Some of my Best Jews are Friends

Why do Baptists object to fornication? Because they're afraid it might lead to dancing. Or try this one for size. The priest says to the rabbi, "When are you going to relax a bit and enjoy a bit of pork?" The rabbi replies laconically, "On your wedding day."

Then there's the story of the rabbi who was complaining about how many of his flock were becoming Quakers. His fellow rabbi agreed. "Some of my best Jews are Friends," he said.

Is it legitimate to make fun of religion? And is making fun of God the ultimate No-No? (H.L. Mencken once described God as "the only comedian whose audience is afraid to laugh.") This is the territory this intrepid column seeks to enter today, at its peril.

Raising this question at a time when the world seems to be full of crazed religious buggers carrying around cruise missiles or envelopes full of anthrax spores may not be entirely prudent. These are times when a humble jobbing satirist can be transported straight to the happy-hunting ground for making a wee joke about Jerusalem, or Jesus Christ, or Allah.

And I think that's a shame. So help me God.

In the post-September 11th situation, when the world's

nerves are jangling, questioning the war out loud becomes an act of treason – especially if you are a New Labour back bencher – and people tread around religious territory as if it were a fire-walk. Nothing must be said which might offend Muslims, Christians or Jews. To do these things is to risk the wrath of people who believe God has appointed them to execute his will, with the emphasis on the word 'execute'.

The warning lights should be flashing. Times of war and national crisis are historically times when individual civil liberties are suspended. Now, dear God, we are to have legislation to crack down on religious hatred. The intentions of the proponents of this legislation are entirely honourable, but the move is full of danger.

When is a statement an expression of bigotry, and when is it an honest disagreement? Which members of the thought police will make that decision? There is a serious danger nowadays that anyone who has strong convictions which conflict with the current consensus will be labelled a bigot.

The churches are, by and large, preposterous institutions. The sight of decrepit geezers in frocks laying down the law about the minutiae of sexual behaviour is beyond parody. Churches can also be kindly institutions. An immense amount of social work is done by churches. And there are church groups which will care for people whom no one else will touch.

Churches can also be dangerous, especially when they are utterly convinced that they are doing the will of God. Consider Jerry Falwell, the American tv evangelist, who has announced that the twin-towers atrocities occurred because God was angry at American tolerance of gays. Subliminal message to gays: we know where you live.

Will making a serious critique of Christians, Muslims and Jews be a hanging offence under the proposed

76

legislation? No. But there is a danger that under an illiberal regime, this kind of law will be used oppressively. I have argued in this column that Islam is a much richer and more sophisticated faith than the stereotypes allow. Nevertheless, some of the statements in the Koran and in Islamic law are ferocious. To refrain from saying this is less than truthful.

Similarly, Judaism is a faith with many virtues. Yet some of its scriptures can be used by Jewish zealots to justify kicking Palestinian ass around the west bank and attempting to redraw territorial boundaries to coincide with ancient biblical maps.

Christianity can produce lives of genuinely heroic quality, but some of its foundational texts can be read as justifying ethnic cleansing. No amount of intellectual handstands can get away from all of this.

Is it offensive to point all this out? If it is, then tough. Quite a number of religious devotees have turned taking offence into an art form. What maddens authoritarians believes more than anything is satire, because it gets under the skin. Laughter is a subversive activity in times of crisis, and is much feared by despots.

Even if it's ok to laugh at religious institutions, surely laughing at God should be a punishable offence? Some people are now arguing that the law of blasphemy should be extended to cover Allah. It shouldn't – it should be abolished altogether. The notion that God needs Ian Paisley, or anyone else, to defend him is preposterous. What we need are changed hearts and minds, not more legislation.

The post-modern satirist is in line with the Old Testament prophets, some of whom – like Socrates – were regarded as atheists because they challenged the consensual understanding of the divine. They saw that there were people who knew more about God than God knew about himself, and that such people were a danger.

Very few things in life should be taken utterly seriously. Most of what we think we know turns out to be a form of idolatry. "Relate thyself relatively to the relative, and absolutely to the Absolute" is Kierkegaard's wise verdict.

Or, as the shaken bishop told his priests, "The good news is that I spoke to God today and everything is ok. The bad news is that she called from Salt Lake City."

It could be you

L ook around you. Study the people in the train compartment, the bus, or the underground. Notice the people in your workplace, in the pub, at the supermarket or on the football terraces. Check out your own family. One in five is really quite a lot.

Yes, one in five Scots either have had, are having, or will have mental illness of one kind or another. That means that one million people in Scotland can expect to suffer mental disorder at some point in their lives. We're not talking about feeling a bit low, or having a few ups and downs, but about afflictions that can range all the way from mild depression to hearing voices in the head urging the killing of little children.

Yes, look around. It could be anyone on that train or subway. You won't be able to tell by looking at them. Dress or social class will give no clue. Mental illness knows no barriers. It could be your boss, your spouse, your son or daughter. Look at yourself in the mirror: it could be you.

Twenty per cent of Scots. The figures were released this week as part of the Scottish Executive's £4m national programme *Well?*, which has been drawn up to tackle mental health issues throughout the country. Health minister Malcolm Chisholm, said, "Mental health should have the same status and understanding as physical diseases and the national programme places it at the centre of the whole health improvement agenda. We need to take a much broader view, where mental health and well-being is accepted as being inextricably linked to good physical health."

The Executive's research indicates that nearly three in 10 employees will have some kind of mental health problem in any one year, costing Scotland between £1bn and £2bn a year in lost business. It also estimates that mental illness is responsible for three in 10 visits to GPs.

One of the most troubling statistics is that rates of suicide in young men have increased by 50 per cent in the past 10 years, while the number of hospital admissions for self-harm have doubled. In Glasgow alone, it is estimated that as many as 33,000 children and young people could have an emotional or mental health problem.

Mental health care has been the Cinderella of the health service for far too long. Mental illness can cause great anguish and distress not only to the sufferers, but to their families and friends. What makes life even harder for the sufferer is the stigma attached to such troubles, even in the 21st century. If a person breaks a leg, he or she can expect to be treated with sympathy, with hilarity, even. Mental sufferers often experience prejudice and rejection.

Mental illness, by its very nature, is an illness of the shadows. Not only is it looked down upon, it is feared. The sufferer need not expect too much in the way of public sympathy. People experiencing depression are often told to pull themselves together, and made to feel it's their own fault. Employees are accused of malingering, and are given a hard time by work colleagues. They are told that their trouble is "all in the mind" – as if that somehow made it easier to bear. Mental and emotional difficulties can cause a person to lose a valued job, and it can be very hard to get back into work.

The reality is that mental illness can strike anyone at any time. It is no respecter of persons. That is why mental illness is so feared, and why sufferers are treated with such insensitivity, derision even. Ridicule and avoidance are ways of keeping unknown, irrational, fears at bay.

We are witnessing in this country an epidemic of burn-out among young people, many of them damaged by the stress of too-long working hours. Sufferers are often unable to get up in the morning, are scared that they're hearing or seeing things, are so worried they can't sleep or eat, or are anxious in case they are going mad.

One in five. It may be you. It may be the person whose cheery wee face is at the top of this column. Some time back, after eight demanding years of ministry in Easterhouse – in the last year of which Superman also wrote a biography through the night – I went on an exchange to a church in Canada. When I got out to the prairies, I crash-landed. I was in a state of exhaustion.

The release of the Easterhouse work pressure allowed waves of depression to sweep through me. I could barely function. Yet I had always been a coper, a doer. My body felt battered, and my messianic self-image took a real pounding. Burnout. I couldn't sleep. In daytime, it was if the world had switched from colour to black and white. Scary.

I was never one to go to the doctor, but I had to. When I told him I felt humiliated, he smiled, and said quietly, "Welcome to the human race". What got me through? Certainly not being told to pull myself together. No, it was support, human and divine. Plus the binning of Superman's cape.

Yes, one in five. Look around you. Look not with eyes of judgement, but of compassion. It could be you. If it is, then welcome to the human race.

Rage, Rage Against the Lightening of the Dye

age, rage against the dying of the light, wrote the
great Dylan after watching his father dying. Thomas
was right: there are things worth raging about.
There are also things not worth losing the plot over. The
woman who assaulted a young hairdresser because her
hairstyling fluids "ran" in the rain was guilty of excess.
Rage, rage, against the lightening of the dye? No, it's not
really worthy of a self-destructive Welsh genius's finest
phrases, is it?

Rage is all the rage. It's everywhere. Road rage. Air rage.
Telephone rage. Trolley rage. It's so fashionable, so cool, so
happening. This week 20-year-old Melanie Andrews from
Hampshire was sentenced to 100 hours of community
service after being convicted of shunting a parked car into
oncoming traffic. She was enraged because another woman
drove into the last parking space at a shopping mall. Her
lawyer told the court that his client had been under pressure.

"It is clear this incident was effectively the straw that
broke the camel's back," said Mr Lowrie, clearly a man
who will leave no stone cliché unturned in the pursuit of
justice. "She chose this moment to exercise some of her
determination not to be pushed around or be told what to

do. It is not a tantrum, it is a manifestation of a great deal welling up in that lady's life."

So that's all right, then.

A court case which has gripped America concerns a wealthy young socialite who reversed her sports car into a crowd, causing death and destruction, after being refused admission to some establishment or other. Probably wasn't a tantrum, more a creative expression of a determination not to be told what to do. Pity about the punters dangling from the bumper, but that's life, isn't it?

Angry about not getting another drink on the plane? Why not stick a bottle in the stewardess's face and end up being wrestled to the floor by the pilot? Ready when you are, pal. Mad about slow service at the till when you're in a hurry? Give the harassed wage-slave a volley of foul-mouthed, vituperative insults. You'll feel better for this colourful manifestation of a great deal welling up in your life. In fact, you'll have successfully transferred a good part of what is welling up in your life on to the hapless girl. But that's what she's paid for, isn't it?

Driving is becoming a more and more unpleasant experience. Simply to be a tad tardy out of the starting blocks when the traffic lights change is to invite manic honking, or the sight of a puce male with throbbing temple veins snarling and jabbing his finger at you. Should you commit the crime of being elderly, the abuse will be worse.

Edinburgh Sheriff Court heard this week how James Reid, a retired consultant, had been driving his new Renault Laguna carefully through tight roadworks in a 40 mph restriction area. He became aware of a transit van on his tail. When traffic slowed down, the driver of the van, John Marsh, shunted the Renault three times, smashing his own headlights. When Mr Reid stepped out of his car to see what damage had been done, he was punched on the side of his head by Marsh, who drove off at speed.

It is not just white van man who is involved in this

kind of stuff. *The Herald* reports that an irate doctor broke a London Underground worker's nose in an attack during a row over train delays.

What is this all about? Enter on left the psychobabble specialists. Professor Ellis Cashmore, who lectures in culture, media and sport at Staffordshire University, blames the increase in violent public rage on the fact that some areas of life have failed to keep pace with the rapid development of technology and communications. The good professor opines, "We just can't speed up some parts of life as we can others, so we need to think creatively how to distract people to take their minds off the waiting, or in some cases just pacify them."

It's just as well we have brilliant professors of sociology to keep us right, or we might fall into the trap of thinking that that a bit of self-discipline might be a good thing. We might be tempted to think that throwing a tantrum when you don't get your own way or when an elderly person holds you up for a nano-second is a sign of astonishing immaturity.

There are lots of stressors in our western civilisation, but compared to times when life was nasty, brutish and short, most of us are privileged. We are not at war. Life expectancy is much higher. Health is much better. On average, we have much greater wealth than our grandparents. Yet we must, it seems, be 'diverted' from our anger if we cannot get what we want, and get it now. If we are to be 'honest' human beings, apparently, we are entitled to vent our rage on whoever gets in the flight path of our precious little lives.

There are things worth raging about, like the fate of millions of children needlessly dying of hunger and disease in a world which has vast resources. Petulant foot-stamping won't change a thing for these children. The channelling of rage against the dying of their lights into serious moral and political choices: now that would represent emotional growing up of a transforming kind.

The Principled, Devouring Presbyterian Beast

Ministers of good things are like torches, a light to others, waste and destruction to themselves.
RICHARD HOOKER, 16th century divine

I t was, one has to say, an impressive funeral service, though not without its ironies. Glasgow Cathedral, filled to capacity. Erstwhile vindictive critics nodding their heads at eloquent tributes to one of Scotland's most admired and best-loved sons. Teary friends standing next to people already plotting the succession. Then out, blinking, into the brightness. The streets beside the Cathedral lined with silent people, some openly weeping. Whatever their background, they had lost a friend.

Yes, the funeral of Geoff Shaw, on May 3, 1978, was quite an occasion. Geoff had been Labour's great white hope, the man who would, or could, be premier. He had obvious personal qualities. He was a Scotsman who seemed born to lead, at a time when huge national opportunities were opening up.

Then one day this energetic 51-year-old man collapsed with a heart attack. Soon, Scotland was in mourning for a lost leader. Aren't we always?

At the time, it looked as if Scotland was on the brink

of achieving home rule. And the name on most pundits' lips as the obvious candidate for first Scottish premier was the Reverend Geoffrey Mackintosh Shaw. When he died, the sense of loss was palpable. Many people who had never met him felt they knew him.

Shaw had spent many years living in the Gorbals as a Church of Scotland minister with an open door – at any time of the day or night – for the lonely, the lost, the drug addicts, the destitute. It was anger against poverty that eventually drove him into politics, and, in his fast-track rise to prominence, he still kept that battered door open for the wandering ones. This complex, heroic, driven, selfless, private, holy, secular, Protestant, Gorbals monk could not let any of it go. And it killed him.

Fast-forward to 1994. A few people are gathered round a grave near Iona Abbey. One of the mourners is Donald Dewar. He has come to say farewell to his friend, John Smith, a Scotsman marked down as Britain's next prime minister, who has died at the grievously young age of 55. The death of Smith, a Kirk elder driven by a passion for social justice, has touched the nation; now his mortal remains are being buried in the rich earth of the historic, windswept resting place of kings and crofters. His grave will become a shrine.

And yesterday, Donald's turn. As the choir sings, I remember how he came to my house in Govan to speak with some friends. It was during Margaret Thatcher's second term, when Labour looked unelectable, and the dream of a Scottish parliament seemed a distant one. Pushed right to the edge of the hairy sofa by our indignantly displaced dog, the wobbling, gesticulating Donald talked with passion about how one day there would be a democratic parliament in Scotland, with social justice at the top of its agenda.

And now, after coming back in frailty to his demanding

desk, he is dead, too. There is a sense of inevitability about it all.

My feelings at these repeated public funerals are deeply ambivalent. These are men I revere, yet they make me angry. Why? Because by not caring enough for themselves, they deprived us, and their loved ones, of them, much too early. Is it simplistic to say that they worked themselves into an early grave? People are too complex to be reduced to one-track explanations; yet self-neglectful compulsiveness unquestionably exacted a terrible price.

In my experience, the principled, devouring, Presbyterian beast has a pathological underbelly. When conscientious Calvinism meets overwhelming Scottish human need, someone, it seems, has to die. The wounds of the body politic have a way of showing up in a stressed, vulnerable human body. How many lost leaders can we mourn, for Christ's sake?

Shaw, Smith, Dewar. From them I wanted their passion, but not their Passion. I wanted their motivation, but not their martyrdom. I wanted their drive, but not their drivenness. I wanted their work, but not their workaholism. I wanted their life for Scotland, but not their death for Scotland. They are truly awesome, truly awful role models.

No. I am sure of this. I do not want my leaders to kill themselves for me, or for anyone else.

And yet, I want to see these terrible heroes justly memorialised: not by post-mortem baubles or bronze statues, but by a Scotland in which everyone, including Geoff Shaw's lost ones, has a rightful place at the table in the feast of life.

Shaw, Smith, Dewar: what a twentieth century apostolic Scottish succession of inspiring leaders who laid waste to their own selves! While I want to refuse their complicit immolations, I also desire to honour the complex heroisms and transcendent virtues of their mortal lives and passions. For them I yearn the resurrection implicit in Geoff Shaw's favourite poem, "Everyone Sang", by Siegfried Sassoon. It was read at Geoff's wedding, less than three years before his death:

> *Everyone suddenly burst out singing;*
> *And I was fill'd with such delight*
> *As prison'd birds must find in freedom*
> *Winging wildly across the white*
> *Orchards and dark green fields; on; on;*
> *And out of sight.*
>
> *Everyone's voice was suddenly lifted,*
> *And beauty came like the setting sun.*
> *My heart was shaken with tears; and horror*
> *Drifted away ... O but everyone*
> *Was a bird; and the song was wordless; the*
> *Singing will never be done.*

What if Hamlet Had Been Called Stan

The setting for the open-air production of *Romeo and Juliet* was wonderful. The lawn in front of Scone Palace, with its high battlements and the wailing of peacocks, made for an atmospheric evening: and all a few yards away from the mound on which several kings of Scotland were crowned. It was a truly Shakespearian setting.

The rain on the journey from Iona abated as we reached Perth, giving way to one of the few fine evenings on mainland Scotland in recent weeks. As the Cutting Edge theatre company are currently discovering, arranging a series of open-air productions in the height of a Scottish summer is a hazardous business.

Scone worked. Some of the action took place among the audience as we sat on the grass. Capulets and Montagues, arrayed in Alison Brown's superb costumes, argued amidst picnic baskets and bottles of wine before getting down to the serious business of stabbing each other.

The hero was suitably handsome, and his teenage love winsome and beautiful. Even as we willed them on to a happier outcome, the two star-crossed lovers moved inexorably towards the destiny we all knew awaited them.

What evocative names! Romeo and Juliet! These names are a byword for love's young dream. But, as the peacocks howled from the trees, I got to thinking: what if their names had been different? Would it matter? What if they had been called Fred and Aggie?

Think of the familiar scene. The pale, love-sick girl stands on the balcony and utters the immortal words: "O Fred, Fred! Wherefore art thou Fred? Deny thy father and refuse thy name. O gentle Fred, if thou dost love, pronounce it faithfully."

Fred: "Sweet Aggie, it is my soul that calls upon my name. How silver-sweet sound lover's tongues by night, like softest music to attending ears."

Aggie: "O Fred, goodnight! Goodnight! Parting is such sweet sorrow, that I shall say goodnight till it be morrow."

Fred and Aggie, the fateful lovers - it's different, isn't it?

And what if Hamlet had been called Stan. Would the melancholy prince have the same gravitas?

Stan: "Was't Stan wrong'd, Laertes? Never Stan: if Stan from himself be tae'n away, and when he's not himself does wrong Laertes, then Stan does it not, Stan denies it."

To be or not to be Stan, that is the question for Hamlet. Now supposing that the great emperor Alexander the Great had been christened Cyril. Cyril the Great doesn't have the same ring about it, does it? You can't imagine someone with a name like Cyril bestriding the known world, can you? It could only be a Monty Python movie, with Cyril played by John Cleese.

Yes, names are strange things. Imagine a thundering Old Testament prophet called Sid. Hector would work OK, but not Sid. And what if the disciples of Jesus had had public school names? "And Jesus saith unto Nigel, get thee behind me Satan." Doesn't work, does it?

Let's take this further. If Jesus had been called Jimmy, it would have all sounded a bit different. "And they took Jimmy out and crucified him". Eh? And the thief on the cross beside him, saying "See you, Jimmy". Surely not. The dynamic is all wrong.

And if the mother of Jesus had been called Doris, Christian history wouldn't have been quite the same. The Virgin Doris? Think about it. Imagine these scriptures being read out in church: "And in the sixth month the angel Gabriel was sent from God unto a city of Galilee named Nazareth, to a virgin espoused to a man whose name was Joseph, of the house of David; and the virgin's name was Doris." Why not? And while I'm at the business of offending everybody, try substituting the name Archie for Mohammed.

There are names that can change the course of history. Take the young German corporal in the First World War, Adolf Schicklgruber. Could he have seized power in Germany with that name? He obviously thought not. He changed his surname to Hitler.

Try it and see what I mean. Put down your *Herald,* stand up, stick your arm out in front of you, click your heels and shout "Heil Schicklgruber!" If you're at home, your dug will be astounded. If you're at work, it will create an interesting diversion in the office. Can you picture 200,000 people at Nuremberg screaming "Heil Schicklgruber!"? Again, it's a John Cleese number.

Changing names might well have been the answer for the two Italians whose problems were reported last week in the press. Giovanni Talluto was born in Palermo on September 3, 1954. So was Giovanni Talluto. One is a barman, and the other is a watchmaker. The problem is that the government can't tell them apart.

When the barman went to the registrars to see about getting married, he was told that he already had a wife. His fiancée was understandably annoyed. "That upset my fiancée more than a little," he told the Sicilian daily, the *Giornale di Sicilia.* "Fortunately, we managed to clear things up pretty quickly."

The barman was issued with a tax bill demanding more than he earned in an entire year. Just two weeks ago he was issued with a speeding ticket even though he doesn't own a car.

The two Giovannis were not aware of each other until they were called up for national service. "The officer called out my name and date of birth and I stood up and said, 'I am Giovanni Talluto'," the barman said. "Then he stood up and said, 'No, I am Giovanni Talluto'."

But in 1994, the barman said, the authorities managed to make a slip that would have more than compensated for all of the confusion. The barman, who had been issued with the same national insurance number as the watch-maker, received notification at 40 that he could retire. A computer had added together the two men's tax contributions.

"It would have been too good to retire at that age. At least for once the anomaly would have been useful for something," he sighed.

Back to Scone palace. The sweet girl puts it all into perspective, as she talks about her lover changing his name. "What's in a name?" she declaims. "That which we call a rose by any other name would smell as sweet."

Aaaw, nice. But you would say that, Aggie, wouldn't you?

In Praise of Family Values

The Highland Park whisky gives free flow to the memory as the evening goes on, and we swap reminiscences and hopes for the future. The couple who are staying with my wife and I are dear, long-standing friends; they are here in Orkney with their twenty-something daughter.

Steve and Jane are one of the finest couples I know. Not only have they been deeply committed to each other for over thirty years, they are impressively generous and compassionate.

Some couples become more introverted as they get older; Steve and Jane have maintained a concern not just for their own family but for the wider community, and have managed to do so in a way which is neither patronising nor self-righteous.

Their Christian convictions, though deep, are never trumpeted. One was brought up in the evangelical Church of Scotland tradition, the other is a Quaker. Their daughter, who is adopted, could not have been brought up in a more caring family environment.

At this point, I must make a confession. While everything else I have written so far is absolutely true, Steve and Jane are not the proper names of our friends. In fact, they are not a man and a woman at all. They are both women. They are a "couple". Has your attitude to them changed in the course of this paragraph?

I will not give you their proper names. To name them would expose them to abuse – especially from Christians. During the poisonous Section 28 debate of unblessed memory, we were invited to see such people as a threat to the very foundations of society. In a number of churches, this Christian couple would be excluded from Holy Communion.

Today, the Adoption of Children Bill will be debated in Westminster. If, after a free vote, it becomes law, unmarried and same-sex couples in England and Wales will be allowed to adopt children. The authorities will, of course, continue to make assessments about the applicants' relationship.

The churches see this as part of a conspiracy against marriage. Is there such a campaign? Actually, I think there is. What we are seeing is not only repeated public examination of the obvious flaws in the institution, but strands of a rampant, full-scale, anti-marriage ideology. The pressures on marriage are now so enormous that it's no wonder that so many collapse under the strain.

There are zealous evangelists out there with a deep hatred of marriage. These anti-marriage fundamentalists, who command a disproportionate amount of air-wave time, insist that, by its very nature, marriage is a prison from which any enlightened person must escape.

So I have some sympathy with the marriage-at-all-costs advocates. They have a case. But where I part company with them is in their attacks on gays.

For some reason, public promoters of "family values" seem to be paranoid about gays. If, as they claim – and the research backs them up – homosexuals represent only about 1% of the population at large, why do they get into such a lather about the matter? After all, gays are hardly closet heterosexuals who are passing up the opportunity of joyful marriage.

To be married is not to be any more or less moral than anybody else. Many people choose cohabitation not out of ideology, but because they are not impressed by the marriages they observe. Some marriages, in fact, provide a disastrous environment in which to bring up children.

My two friends have brought up their adopted daughter with great love, care and respect, teaching her the values they themselves try to live out. The biggest threats to marriages come not from gays, but from casual and exploitative heterosexual sex, along with the anti-human, long-hours pressures of the workplace.

If the institution of marriage can only be shored up by attacking gays and cohabitees, there is something seriously wrong. Where the debate becomes truly vicious is when a link between homosexuality and paedophilia is implied. The statistics show this to be nothing but a smear – yet that smear is repeated shamelessly in religious debate.

I know that I'm in a minority here, but I'm ashamed of the way in which churches have dealt with gay people. Homosexuality is a troublesome, unasked-for endowment, not a moral choice. Promiscuity, not orientation, is the destabilising problem. To demonise those who are trying to live their sexual lives with integrity is a disgrace.

To say this kind of thing in the church is to be regarded as a traitor, someone who is letting the side down. Issues about sexuality produce more aggressive fury in churches than any other matter. "Liberal" is used as a contemptuous epithet. It so happens that I'm liberal on some issues and conservative on others, but that is by the by. In my experience, both liberals and conservatives have a "pick and mix" attitude to the scriptures; indeed, grown-up thinking demands that this be so.

Ethics has to do with the way in which people treat

each other. If I were to perform a ceremony of blessing for my two friends, I would be in serious trouble. Yet if I were to bless a nuclear submarine, carrying enough fire-power in its belly to incinerate millions of men, women and children in a space of minutes, I would feel no ecclesiastical finger on my collar.

Family values? Give me a break.

A Deadly Serious Business

Sven-Goran Eriksson, manager of England, said in a *Herald* interview this week that he was encouraging his players to relax. "It's dangerous to think about football and do nothing else all day," he commented. "The pressure is always here with us. That's as it should be. However, you should force yourself to forget about it now and again. You should try to have a laugh. Life is fun."

So what does the bold Sven do for a laugh, for fun? Not unsurprisingly, he doesn't mention a spot of Swedish massage with Ulrika Jonson. "I do some running, and I am already reading a Swedish book about alternative diets. It's interesting."

Aye, right. What does the football professor do when he wants to be serious?

Now, either you found the interview with the England manager funny, or not. Sven certainly didn't mean it to be. Humour, like beauty, lies in the eye of the beholder. This means you can find it pretty well everywhere.

But is everywhere OK? Is it permissible, for instance, to laugh at individual people? Here's another real-life example: a hapless English performer of theatrical legend put everything into winning over the notoriously difficult audience of the Glasgow Metropole. He tried jokes, songs, and then dance. All his attempts met with silence.

In desperation, the entertainer took out his trumpet.

"My God!" came the cry from the gods. "Is there nae end to your fucking talent?"

Is it funny? Yes. As usual with Glasgow, the best comedians had paid to get in. The death of the poor entertainer with his boots on got the biggest laugh of the night. He wasn't laughing, though: crying, perhaps.

Take this further: is it acceptable to laugh at other races? What about stories about Jews? In fact, the best ones are told by Jewish comedians. Is disability OK for a bit of fun? Billy Connolly would say yes. What are the borderlines, the no-go areas? Are there any?

What prompts this reflection is the new comedy series, *Six Feet Under* which began on Channel 4 this week. Written by Alan Ball, who scripted American Beauty, the series gets its laughs in a strange place – a mortuary. In this it follows in the tradition of such books as Nancy Mitford's *The American Way of Death*, Evelyn Waugh's *The Loved One*, and Alan Spence's *Way to Go*.

Six Feet Under tells the story of the Fisher family who run a funeral parlour. Within a few minutes, you know that this is a truly dysfunctional family. The authoritarian father, Nathaniel Fisher, who is going through a midlife crisis, is killed in his brand new Cadillac hearse on Christmas Eve. The oldest son, Nate jnr, gets the news on his mobile phone as he is finishing having sexual intercourse with a women he has met on a plane. The youngest child, Claire, is told just seconds after she has inhaled some crystal meth, which will make everything much more lurid.

The family which deals in death turns out to be unable to cope when death comes home. They are dealing with corpses all the time, but this particular corpse throws them into hysterical disarray. As the scenario unfolds, there is lots of humour, but it is very, very black. It is a promising series.

Death is a taboo subject. One way to bring a nice little dinner party to a silent conclusion would be to point out quietly, just before the desert, that within thirty years everyone round the table will be dead. Funny? It's hilarious. It has a nice Kierkegaardian ring. Discussion over the liqueurs might be a little stilted, as the guests get mentally prepared to go out into the long, dark night.

There are many funny aspects to death and the disposal of bodies. The reality is, though, that the humour around the subject is there because it's too difficult a topic to confront head on. Ye laugh for ye maun daurna cry. The knowledge of our inevitable mortality and the anxiety that accompanies the hard fact of unavoidable death are routinely pushed to the background of human consciousness. As Woody Allen puts it: "It is impossible to experience one's own death objectively and still carry a tune."

It is part of the human condition to live as if death were something that happened to other people. Allen said he knew that all men were mortal, but he always supposed that an exception would be made in his case. He added that he didn't want to achieve immortality through his work – he wanted to achieve it by not dying.

When all the jokes are set aside, death is a deadly serious business. It can be sent up, but not sent away. Human beings have to take up an attitude to their own death. The real freedom to laugh comes not when death is pushed away, but when it is faced with faith: laughter is one of the characteristics of resurrection. It is possible to carry a hymn tune.

In the meantime, humour about death is good – at least, when it's genuinely funny, rather than strained. Back to that irreverent Jew, Woody Allen: "It's not that I'm afraid to die, I just don't want to be there when it happens."

The Sash my Lawyer Wore

Claret-drinking Tory Egyptologists from Cowdenbeath are, one has to say, an endangered species. In fact, only one of them has ever been spotted. This week, on the radio, he confessed that in the wee small hours of a very dark morning in his life, he came very close to rendering the species extinct.

Donald Findlay's well-earned reputation as one of Scotland's most brilliant defence counsels made him first choice for anyone facing life imprisonment. An expert on the pyramids – was it the coal bings of Cowdenbeath that first gave him the notion? – the flamboyant Findlay became a leading light in the Scottish Conservative party as well as vice chairman of Rangers Football Club. He was a charismatic performer on the stage of Scotland's public life, with everything to play for.

Yet two years ago, as Findlay told Muriel Gray on her programme *Before you go* (an imaginative series in which public figures are confronted with their make-believe obituaries), this flamboyant high flyer sat in his flat in the early morning gloom with suicide pills in front of him. What had undone him, as we all know, was being caught on someone's video camera singing such elevated legal arias as "The Sash my father wore" at a party to celebrate Rangers' feat in winning the treble.

I found the accused's radio defence this week to be

pretty lame. These were football songs, he said, and it was a football supporters' party. Come on, Donald, you can do better than that. Given the history of sectarian tension in the west of Scotland, the sight of one of Scotland's best known lawyers belting out lyrics about Fenian blood was both unedifying and explosive. It was a self-inflicted wound which sadly tapped into a much wider and more dangerous west of Scotland wounding.

His plea that many others have done it before him is no defence, as he must know. Given his public willingness to take unpopular stances, a high-profile personality with the forcefulness and eloquence of Findlay could have provided leadership in the campaign to change the sectarian mindset.

In fact, I believe that Donald Findlay can yet provide that high quality leadership, particularly after his chastening experience. He is no bigot, and he has a track record to prove it. He is also a man of private kindness. Let me give you one small example. After Cowdenbeath football club's stand was burned down – were the thieves looking for the trophy room? – Findlay promised to bring through a Rangers side to open the new stadium and raise funds for the struggling club. He was as good as his word. He has done other unpublicised things to raise funds for local young players.

His grandstanding High Court defence performances have been brilliant reminders of the foundation stone of our justice system – that the accused is innocent until the state has proved him guilty. And he was such a good rector of St Andrews University and powerful spokesman for the underdog that the students elected him for two terms.

What I found most touching about Findlay's public confession was the revelation that his public persona is a façade, covering up a "terrible, terrible profound shyness" and lack of personal confidence.

"I just have this great fear of people getting too close, people seeing you for your weaknesses," he said. "If you are basically very shy, the one thing you don't want people to realise is that you are shy, because then you feel discomfited and it becomes self-perpetuating."

Donald Findlay is a big enough man to recover from all this, and I hope that his great gifts will not be permanently lost to Scottish public life. He would bring a sparkle to the Scottish parliament.

Earlier in the week another very able man, also known to me, admitted on air his vulnerability and his inability to cope. David Ogston, minister of the Church of St John the Baptist, Perth, is one of the Church of Scotland's brightest and best. He is an outstanding minister and a fine poet.

On BBC Radio Scotland's excellent Sunday morning sequence – which deservedly has a large listening audience – Ogston told how one Sunday morning his life suddenly became dizzyingly destabilised. As he stood at the communion table, trying to find his balance, his body was speaking to him. The message was that his life could not continue as normal.

His pride was hurt. He was, was he not, a man who could cope? Now, this public figure could no longer carry on in public. This highly articulate son of a crofter had to go private, to look at his own wounding, to find salvation in the rich brown earth of his own garden.

Like Donald Findlay's story, David Ogston's reflections – which continue for another two weeks – point to the hidden vulnerability which lies at the heart of many public figures. Because we are so used to hype and spin and caricature, we easily forget that most of us are multi-levelled, complex, beings.

Two years ago, one could not have imagined either of these strong figures making such a confession. Perhaps we should read about the people who inhabit the front pages of our newspapers with much more compassion in our hearts. We do not know what private burdens they carry. Far too often it's only when we read the real obituaries that we begin to understand.

Sometimes it's hard to be a Man

H ere is a joke. Whether you find it funny or not will depend on where you're coming from. The airline captain announces that there is something wrong with the engines, and that the plane will crash in five minutes. What to do in the last few minutes of life? An attractive blonde at the front of the cabin stands up and says, in a loud voice, "I would like a man who will make me feel like a woman".

All eyes turn to the back of the plane as a handsome, bronzed young man steps to his feet. There is a frisson in the air as he takes his jacket off and starts to walk down the aisle. His tie comes off next, while the blonde smiles adoringly. As he draws nearer, the man starts to unbutton his shirt. With a dramatic gesture he whips it off. Then he hands the garment to the young woman. "Iron this," he says.

Most women would want to kill a man who told this story. It's the kind of joke/reality that launched the feminist movement. Its very crassness would prevent many men from repeating the joke in mixed company, either because they were repelled by it, or out of fear of sustaining grievous bodily harm.

Sometimes, though, it's hard to be a modern man. Research published yesterday claims that in the post-

feminist age, there is simply no right way for men to be-
have. Just at the point at which we've learned to be in
touch with the inner feminine, cry, wash the dishes, refrain
from holding the door open for women and control the
urge to stand up for ladies on the bus, it seems that it's all a
bit of a mistake. Well, most of it.

The research, commissioned by Lloyds TSB Private
Banking and carried out by The Future Foundation, reveals
that 91per cent of women actually like having the door
held open for them. This is a truly devastating statistic. And
as many as 22 per cent of women are happy that men
should foot the bill for dates. Apparently, young and older
people were most likely to think men should pay for a meal
out.

Men who were brought up to offer their seat on the bus
to a standing lady do so in fear and trembling. The stories
of crushing humiliation are legion. Yet some women, apparently still like it. And nearly all believe that people
should give up their seats for the elderly.

Melanie Howard of research group The Future Foundation said: "It's practically impossible for men to get it right.
Although on the surface the figures for holding open doors
for women seem pretty non-contentious, it still means that
every 10th woman a man steps aside for is probably going
to take offence, which is a pretty daunting thought."

Here is the problem for a modern man. He has fought
all his conditioned tendencies to open doors for women.
Then he learns that, after all, most women prefer it that
way. When he reverts to his old courteous habits, and
holds the door open, nine out of ten women give him a big
smile. Then the tenth leaves him a quivering wreck after a
blistering verbal onslaught. Oh dear.

Here is a further piece of confusion: the popularity of a
book called *The Surrendered Single: A Practical Guide
toAttracting and Marrying the Man Who's Right for You.*

According to author Laura Doyle, who argues that surrendering control means going back to pre-feminist ideas of womanhood. To attract a mate, apparently, single women should smile at every man they meet, always wear form-fitting clothes and make-up, and give "sincere thanks or a compliment to at least one male a day".

Doyle says that being quiet on a date allows the man to impress the woman and makes her seem more feminine, a must for the surrendered creed. She does allow women to communicate their desires in two scenarios: if the man asks for their opinion, or if he suggests doing something that would put her in emotional or physical distress. Otherwise, their feelings are irrelevant.

Aaargh! Something tells me that this is different from Jo Brand's view of men: "The useless piece of flesh at the end of a penis is called a man." Or Roseanne Barr's: "I don't think women want to be equal to men. I think we'd have to have lobotomies to do that. There isn't any New Man. The New man is the old man, only he whines more."

No wonder so many modern men have identity crises, or end up as recluses. Is it to be deference or defiance, mystery or mastery? And is it ever possible to be right? "Don't argue with your mate in the kitchen," advises Diane Amos, "because we know where everything is and you don't."

Here is a joke. Whether you think it funny or not depends on where you're coming from.

Question: How can you tell when a man's had an orgasm?
Answer: You can hear him snoring.
Question: What's the difference between a man and a chimpanzee?
Answer: One is hairy and smelly and is always scratching his rear. And the other's a chimpanzee.

Ach, well. It's good to know that women don't like politically incorrect jokes. Yes, sometimes it's hard to be a man.

Breaking Through the Stained Glass Ceiling

R ight then. Your starter for ten. "Who was the last woman Moderator of the General Assembly of the Church of Scotland?"

You've got it in one. There hasn't been a first woman Mod, never mind a last. As *The Herald* revealed yesterday, a report to be published next month asks how it is that 33 years after the ordination of the first woman to the Kirk's ministry, no female has been appointed to the top job. The report, titled "The Stained Glass Ceiling: Engendering Debate", not only looks at key appointments, but examines the experience of women in ministry. Produced by the Kirk's Gender Attitudes Project, the report is bound to trouble the waters.

This column has already collected bruises in the Kirk's gender wars. It has been clubbed maniacally by normally placid men in frocks for asking why there has never been a female Moderator. My highly paid team of researchers has been out interviewing some of the finest minds in our civilisation. Our "Why, oh why?" question has elicited four deeply moving reasons.

1. There aren't any women who're good enough. This argument has about as much credibility as the reply that Rangers' management used to give in the olden days (ten or so years ago): "We're not biased against Roman Catholics – we simply can't find any Catholic who's good enough to play for us." Honest, your Honour.

2. It doesn't matter anyway. In one way this is true. There are more important things for the Church to get excited about. (I'd imagine that the very mention of Church of Scotland makes God yawn. And that's on a good day.) It may be argued that the Moderatorial office is only symbolic. But symbols matter, especially in this age of mass communication. What kind of signal is the Kirk giving out? Its theoretical position is that men and women are equal in all offices of the Church. How come – after all this time – the Kirk's chief symbolic office would appear to be open only to men of a certain age?

3. It's the Holy Spirit who chooses Moderators. So far, in His inscrutable wisdom, He has only chosen men. The Holy Spirit is the great trump card, to be pulled from out of the sleeve when the going gets really desperate. This ace is beloved of unstoppable zealots and crazed committee conveners. How dare one argue against the Holy Spirit?

Let's remind ourselves of some of the things the Holy Spirit is supposed to have advocated in the past. Witches should be stoned to death. Slavery is the will of God. Women should not be allowed to teach. (Putting that rule into effect today would do for Sunday Schools what BSE and foot-and-mouth has done for the meat trade.) Why do people keep playing the Holy Spirit card to cover up theological laziness?

4. Er, that's it.

Correct.

Isn't it time the Kirk brought its action in line with its theology? This is not an argument for minority quotas. I'm not pleading for a one-legged lentil-eating lesbian Moderator, followed by a black vegetarian midget with a club foot, followed by a transvestite ex-Mormon lap-dancing

Moderator. All this would undoubtedly make the General Assembly much more interesting: but I'm simply asking that when the Church makes key choices it doesn't exclude half the human race. This has nothing to do with "political correctness", but about good theology.

Lurking at the back of all of this are some very dodgy clerical attitudes to women. This goes very, very deep. The greatest of Catholic theologians, St Thomas Aquinas, averred that woman was a freak of nature: "As regards the individual nature, woman is defective and misbegotten." Well, that's youse telt. Female bodies, particularly menstruating ones, have always been a problem for religious males. And sex. Read some classical theological texts and you will find hatred of the body, hatred of sex, and hatred of women running through them.

At the time of the debate over the ordination of women in the Church of England, I heard, with my own lugs, a vicar say, "We'll be ordaining monkeys next". This echoes Samuel Johnson's view: "Sir, a woman preaching is like a dog's walking on his hinder legs. It is not done well: but you are surprised to find it done at all."

In the Roman Catholic Church, the Pope has forbidden even the discussion of the possibility of the ordination of women. One of the arguments is that since Christ was a man, so must the Church's priests. Presumably they should also be Jewish, circumcised and crucified at the age of 33. To cut all this great theology down to its core, it would appear that in order to handle the bread and the wine, one must have – how can I put this with the delicacy for which this worthy column is famed? – a willie.

Women ministers are, thankfully, here to stay in Scotland. I think the stained glass ceiling will soon be breached. Things do change: look again at Rangers Football Club. Nowadays, there are more people crossing themselves at Ibrox than at Lourdes. Remember you read it first in *The Herald*.

The Arithmetic of Disgrace

This week, Dr Rowan Williams, heid man of the Anglican communion, planted his feet firmly under the sacred desk at Canterbury. There is genuine excitement about this bold appointment. Today, the Church of Scotland's "Task Force for Change" will meet at the headquarters of the national Kirk in Edinburgh. Excitement is easily containable. Of its 37 members, how many are women and young people? Read on, Macduff.

In conversation recently with a prominent theologian working in England, I asked him about Williams. "He's the most intellectually gifted man to become Archbishop of Canterbury since St Anselm," the good professor replied unequivocally.

Now that is quite a tribute. For those of you who fall into a coma at the mere mention of matters ecclesiastical, let me explain. Anselm, the most brilliant man of his day, ascended to the see of Canterbury in the year 1093. He wasn't just the Brain of Britain, he was the brain of the known world. His was the most luminous intellect between St Augustine and St Thomas Aquinas. (Pity he was beaten in the race for the title of Greatest Briton by Princess Di and John Lennon.)

Anselm produced his famous "ontological argument" for the existence of God which still engages philosophers to this day. It is so complex that I would go into an altered state of consciousness simply trying to explain it to myself, never mind to gentle readers of this edifying column. It reminds me of the entirely estimable Rev Iain Mackenzie's regular – and not to be missed – erudite message to the nation in the early hours of New Year's morning: if you understood it, it meant that you were completely pissed.

Even when sober, Rowan Williams understands the ontological argument. Yet, if I were him, I would beware of hyperbolic comparisons. I suspect that he does. He should also be alarmed by a good press. Any man who is canonised by the *Guardian* should walk in fear of the *Sun,* that not-so-holy ghost which will haunt the feast when Canterbury tales are told.

He is an orthodox theologian who has never hidden his radical views. A man of genuine holiness, he once chanted psalms on the runway of a military base as a theological protest against nuclear weapons. Surprisingly for a high churchman, he has consistently supported the ordination of women, and has declared that he sees no barriers to the consecration of woman bishops. He is sympathetic to gays. He is known to be uncomfortable with the trappings of ecclesiastical establishment. (It is ironic that in Scotland, begowned and bejewelled presbyterian church leaders look more and more like prelates at a time when the monkish Anglican leader is disinvesting himself in a new and fascinating dance of the seven episcopal veils.) No wonder the knives are already out for him.

At 52, Rowan Williams is at the height of his powers. As one who has read much of his theological work, I can say for sure that this man will cause waves in the Church of England and well beyond. The big question is whether the Welshman will be able to see through the reforms he wants, or whether he will be suffocated by the Anglican establishment. The fact that he has not trimmed and tacked in order to win high office puts him in a strong position; even so, one should not underestimate the powers which surround the episcopal throne. He may suffer ecclesiastical death by a thousand coughs.

But, I hear you cry impatiently, what about the Kirk's task force for change? Faced by decline over the last fifty years, the Kirk has had the Committee of Forty, the Anderson Committee, The Church Without Walls report, and Harry Reid's Outside Verdict. Not a lot has happened. At the last general assembly, its response was to set up yet another committee.

Given the fact that the Kirk talks a good game about the importance of the eldership, young people, and women, one might reasonably be led to expect that these key areas would be fully represented on this critical new commission. Well, this column can reveal the arithmetic of disgrace. Out of 37 members, 30 are ministers. How many young people? None. How many women? One. Even though two thirds of the church membership is made up of women.

Do these people never learn anything? The make-up of the task force illustrates the problem, not the solution. It represents a section of the Kirk talking to itself. I despair. The many good people in the Kirk deserve better than this. I hope that members will read this column and get really, really mad.

In the past, some people in the Church of Scotland have tended to be a bit sniffy about the Anglican communion. Now, after the shameful timidity over the recent Moderatorial election, we see, over the border, a bold and imaginative turbulent priest ascend to the see of Canterbury. May God go with him.

Ron Ferguson is Dead!

How's that for a cheery headline? Although I'm a fairly laid back kind of guy, the news that I was deid was, I have to admit, a bit of a shock to me. Oscar Wilde said that the first thing he did in the morning was to check the *Times* obituaries, and if his name wasn't there, he got up.

The first thing I did was to check my pulse. At first, alarmingly, I couldn't detect anything. The newspapers must be right! But then I found a faint throb. Something was happening. Me. I was happening, even if faintly. The Kierkegaard of Kirkwall was still breathing, and lived to fight another day.

As word of my demise spread around the civilised world, my friends became greatly alarmed, especially those I owed money to. The switchboard of the electronic croft went into meltdown. I waited for a televised announcement that rumours of my death had been greatly exaggerated, but Mark Twain was no more and there was a war, or something, on. So a grieving nation continued to believe that the electronic crofter had been translated to heaven.

People fainted in the streets of Orkney when I went out. A tractor bearing neeps careered into a ditch. I tell you, there's nothing quite like coming back from the dead to give a man an extra 'edge' in the authority stakes.

Then I read the paper more closely. It turned out to be a different Ron Ferguson! It was Major Ron Ferguson, father of Sarah Ferguson, the former Duchess of York. People who had already prepared eloquent tributes to me – soaring, beautiful eulogies which would have moved whole congregations to sobbing hysteria – were absolutely beeling when they found out that all their time and effort had been wasted. Still, that's the way life goes sometimes.

I always had a bit of a fellow feeling for Major Ron Ferguson. People often confused the two of us. I would get invitations in the post to the coronations of minor European royals. I usually went. Travel broadens the mind, and the food was always great. I would be asked how Sarah was doing, and I would make some sensational stuff up.

The Major, on the other hand, was flattered to be thought to be the author of such distinguished academic tomes as *Donald Dewar Ate my Hamster* and *Hitler was a Vegetarian*. He was particularly pleased when royalties for these books, as well as fees for newspaper articles, were paid into his bank account. He just laughed when I asked him about it. The man had a marvellous sense of humour.

Major Ron even had people asking him how Cowdenbeath football team was doing. His stock reply was that they were about to be relegated, which was usually right. Life got more difficult for him, though, when angry people started accosting him in London streets and saunas, accusing him of writing vulgar articles in *The Herald*. One furious woman even beat him about the head with an umbrella. He had to issue press releases denying that he was the real Ron Ferguson.

It got even more confusing. Other people thought that Major Ron Ferguson was my father. But no, I can say categorically that Fergie and I are not brother and sister. We did not share forbidden childhood secrets (I'll suck your toe if you suck mine). I wish to declare, once and for all, that I have absolutely no connection with La Fergiana. So, if she hassles you in the street, don't phone me to complain. I won't be in.

All of this got me thinking about ontological matters. How do you know that it's me, Ron Ferguson, writing this column? Have you ever thought about that? How do you know that it's not Salman Rushdie? Ah, you reply, the photograph. But how can you be sure that Mr Rushdie hasn't had plastic surgery?

Life is a precarious business. For all you know, that nice, clean-shaven young man who recently moved into your street might be Osama bin Laden with a make-over. Think about it and tremble. You'll never look at your neighbour in the same way again.

Saddam Hussein has about a hundred look-alikes. The fake-Saddams have to taste their boss's food, in case it is poisoned. So every time they sit down to dinner in the presidential palace, they don't know if they'll survive the first course. A bit like eating in some restaurants I know.

What about the wife of a dummy who had plastic surgery? She hadn't bargained for being married to a Saddam lookalike. Maybe the guy lying next to her in the bed actually is Saddam Hussein. Still, her real husband will have a good pension – that is, if he survives dinner, or American missiles. Come to think of it, even British servicemen are lucky if they survive American missiles.

As Ron Ferguson and I used to say to each other: do you know who you are? Have you got proof? After reading these discombobulating reflections, you might want to lie down for the rest of the day. This postmodern column is the thinking person's time bomb. Bet you're glad that Ron Ferguson is alive and well.

The Family that Bokes Together Yokes Together

S o living in the country can literally drive you mad. A report published this week has found that townsfolk who move to the countryside to escape the strains of city living can end up more miserable than before. Researchers say that more than half of those who choose the rural idyll in an attempt to relieve mental stress find their dream turns into a nightmare.

The joint study by academics at Glasgow and Dundee universities destroys the popular myth that rural and island life offers the perfect antidote to fast and furious city life. Remoteness and isolation can exacerbate stress levels and take people all the way to insanity.

Your serene electronic crofter is, of course, exempt from this. True, this column has, from time to time, received letters from *Herald* readers suggesting community care might be appropriate – this very week one reader described me as "completely bonkers" after writing about the death of Ron Ferguson – but these observations are affectionate rather than clinical. *(Are you sure? – Ed.)*

The point of the report, though, is a serious one. People do retreat to remote areas in order to escape the pressures of urban life. During Orkney's glorious summer last year, many visitors commented on how much they would like to live here. The spring weather so far this year has had many delights, and Orkney does feel like the Garden of Eden when the sun in shining.

But when the breezes become less than balmy, do the white settlers become barmy? Some undoubtedly do. Many "ferryloupers" move to Orkney – accompanied by great hopes and a single goat – after having visited the northern isles on a stunning summer's day. Some will have sold their city home for good money and bought a place in rural Orkney having viewed the croft only on the internet.

Then comes the winter. Now I actually enjoy winter here – most of the time – but it's definitely character-building stuff. You soon find out why so many farm buildings are anchored to the ground. We're talking serious wind here. There are days when people weighing less than 15 stones don't leave the house in case they end up in Bergen.

While it is wonderful to witness the awesome power of nature, sailing across the Pentland Firth in a force eight is not for the fainthearted. The first couple of times we came here on a summer family holiday, we were sick. (The only reason Noah endured the stench on the Ark was because he saw the size of the waves outside.) The adversity bonded us. The family that bokes together yokes together. *(Is this meant to be evidence of normality? – Ed.)*

Yes, the island or rural summer idyll looks different in the winter. The darkness of the days takes its toll. SAD (Seasonally Affective Disorder) can make people depressed, and some of those who succumb to the condition titled Morbidis Orcadiensis are people who sought the good life and got more than they bargained for.

Moving to an island or a remote rural area in order to get away from stress may seem appealing while sitting nose-to-tail in traffic on the M8, but it is not for everybody. Rural life has its own stresses, and it is romanticism to think otherwise. After a while in relative isolation, the

116

stress-filled city can suddenly seem very alluring once more.

Fleeing to the isles as a way of dealing with personal problems is not a wise move. Island life puts pressure on people, and the self you tried to escape from in the crowded, urban community will be there to meet you, round the first corner in the country. Angst knows no frontiers. Alcoholics know well the illusory nature of the "geographical cure" – the notion that if only you can move to somewhere else, your problems will disappear. The sad traffic of older, wiser people, with goat, back south, gives the lie to that notion.

I don't wish to exaggerate all this, though. Life on the edge of the known universe has many, many compensations and attractions. Having lived in towns and cities for a good part of my life, I wouldn't exchange the electronic croft in Orkney for a mansion in the central belt.

I enjoy going back to mainland Scotland now and again, especially to see family and dear friends. I like the buzz of the city, and journalism and broadcasting bring me down. And the football, which I miss. This weekend, it so happens, I will be numbered among the faithful at the Stadium of Light, Central Park. Cowdenbeath v Brechin City: what more could a human being wish? *(You clearly have Mad Cowdenbeath Disease as well. – Ed.)*

The Blue Brazil, rooted at the bottom of the Second Division, will make a last-gasp, heroic bid to avoid relegation. Even a diehard loyalist like myself fears that it may simply be a melancholy twitching of the corpse. *(Ron, you've been reading too much Kierkegaard up there in the dark.)*

Then I will head back north via the BBC in Glasgow. After crossing the Pentland Firth, I will inhale the fresh air deep into my lungs, before heading for the deepest Orkney countryside. And I will be glad. *(And possibly a little mad? – Ed.)*

A Diamond Theological Geezer

H ere is your tie-breaker question for this column's
regular festive season quiz. What do Rikki Fulton,
Jonathan Swift, St Dionysius the Pseudo-
Areopagite, and Soren Kierkegaard have in common? You
don't know? Well, I'm not going to tell you. At least, not
until near the end of the column. No, do not go there yet.
Do not pass Go. Do not collect £200.

First of all, some clues. We'll begin with the improbably-named St Dionysius the Pseudo-Areopagite. Who he?
He was a brilliant mystical theologian who knocked
around the known world at the beginning of the sixth
century.

Dionysius – he was only a pseudo Areopagite because
he was confused with your actual Dionysius the Areopagite
mentioned in the New Testament (Acts 17 verse 34), but
you'll know all this anyway – was famous because of the
unusual way he talked about God. He said it was important to know first of all what God was not like. For instance, God is not an old man with a grey beard, God does
not talk like George Bush, God is neither a man nor a
woman, God does not support Rangers or Celtic, and so
on. Once you've stopped babbling foolishly about the
inside-leg measurements of your domesticated God, the
decks have been cleared for the kind of chaste talk about

divine reality which leaves plenty of scope for mystery and not-knowing.

(This edifying column takes no prisoners, by the way. No dumbing-down for us. Readers will recall that we recently discussed St Anselm's ontological argument for the existence of God, which is only understood today by Rowan Williams and Patrick Moore – the mad BBC guy whose right eyebrow goes up and down.)

Next up is Jonathan Swift, born in 1667, Dean of St Patrick's Cathedral, Dublin. A dazzling storyteller, poet and satirist, Swift sent up politics and church with great style and wit. He was never your man for the consensus view, and his independence of mind got him into a lot of trouble. A diamond theological geezer, in fact.

Søren Kierkegaard, born 1813, was another brilliant character who spent most of his time dodging flak from the philosophical and religious establishment of his day. Anticipating the post-modern view, the great Dane argued that the certainties taken for granted by church, university and state were built upon very shaky foundations. He was not thanked for pointing out that the emperor's clothes were cheap hand-me-downs.

And Rikki Fulton? The book about his great comic creation, the Reverend I M Jolly, is currently topping the Scottish bestseller lists. *How I found God, and why He was hiding from me* brings more adventures of the dreary Scottish minister. Tony Roper's book has some great lines in it, but you need to give it the great man's mournful delivery to make it work.

Hogmanay won't be the same without Rikki, who is now, sadly, suffering from Alzheimer's disease. His motorbike cop was a marvel; but all it took was for the lights to dim and the gloomy figure of I M Jolly to appear in the famous chair for Scotland to go into paroxysms of helpless laughter.

Fulton's brilliant caricature of the coma-inducing cleric is a glorious piece of religious satire. (I was interested to read in the book that my favourite *Last Call,* where the meenister, drinking spiked water, becomes more and more incoherent, was not done in the name of I M Jolly but his precursor, the Reverend David Goodchild.) Rikki Fulton, who has been a devoted member of the Church of Scotland for years, rightly sees no contradiction in sending up the Kirk's most banal features.

One of the lugubrious I M Jolly's greatest achievements was to make it almost impossible for any self-respecting cleric to do *Last Call.* Everything is on the edge of parody. I was once inveigled into doing *Reflections* for Grampian TV from St Magnus Cathedral. Seeking to do something subtle, I had the Kirkwall hangman's ladder brought down from the triforium. The sophisticated point I intended to make was that the now-much-sentimentalised cross of Christ was actually the sign of an execution of an outlaw.

The problem was that my cadaverous appearance in the evening light, along with the hangman's ladder, engendered a state of terror in the elderly viewing audience. Not even industrial-strength Horlicks could induce sleep after that. Most of those who survived are still in therapy. I was never invited back.

So what do all these diverse characters, historical and contemporary, have in common? You've won the prize: they are all religious iconoclasts. They are anarchic troublers from within, using humour, questioning, and satire to dismantle false certainties and create a little space where less domineering but more captivating truths may be whispered.

I love all these rumbustious, unsettling, witty fechters. On this Boxing Day, I gladly raise a glass to them and to you, gentle readers of this elevating column. And I invite you to spare a special thought for the wonderful Rikki Fulton, and his wife Kate, at this difficult time.

The Global Hypnotist-Priests in Armani Suits

H i ho, Hi ho, it's back to work we go! Yes, the holidays are well and truly over, and schools are into full flow. But then, like me, you may not have had a holiday. I never go away in the summer – I'm too busy marrying people, and jolly things like that (though it's hard work watching people say "Read my lips – I'll stay with you forever", followed by the risking of repetitive joke injury on the wedding reception rubber chicken circuit).

Summer breaks are supposed to refresh you, and re-charge the batteries. Holidays began as 'holy days' – special days for festive celebration and spiritual refreshment. Now that such things have been largely abandoned, a new and scary secular puritanism has taken over. You see, for in-creasing numbers of people, essential pieces of holiday kit are the laptop computer and the mobile phone.

While on cheapo winter deals abroad recently, I've noticed more and more people talking into their mobile phones while lying on the beach. A lot of them are obvi-ously checking with the office back home. Hey, modern technology's a great thing!

Here's the rub. The new technology was supposed to

liberate us. It was going to make us so efficient that we'd be able to work shorter hours, and even jobshare so that we could have more family time. In our dreams.

The laptop with the holiday luggage represents a form of wired-up slavery. The omnipresent mobile phone means that even though you're at the uttermost ends of the earth, the boss is only a nano-second away. Never fear, a text message will seek you out in the jungle.

Besides, you'd better keep checking that you've still got a job. And while you're at the laptop – finishing off that report that you didn't have time to complete before you left – you might as well read your e-mails. Some of them sound urgent, so it seems a good idea to answer them. Besides, checking in every day will impress your superiors, who know a good slave when they meet one. All this will probably put your blood pressure up. Oh happy day!

Britain now has the longest working hours in Europe. And the highest divorce rate. Read my lips – I'll stay with you till work us do part. Super-efficient technology means that even when you stagger back home, there is no escape. You are reachable by e-mail, text message, fax or phone. Well, it's good to talk, isn't it?

The Psalmist says of Yahweh: "Whither shall I go from thy spirit? Or whither shall I flee from thy presence? If I ascend up into heaven, thou art there: if I make my bed in hell, behold thou art there. If I take the wings of the morning, and dwell in the uttermost part of the sea; even there shall thy hand lead me, and thy right hand uphold me."

What a liberated society we live in! We have overthrown the notion of a divine guiding presence, as well as banishing from our common memory some of the most exquisite prose-poetry the world has ever known; and we have enthroned in their place the electronic omnipresence of the baleful boss, plus semi-literate text messages. Whoopee!

A recent BBC poll showed that one in five workers in the UK is being forced sign an opt-out from the EU working hours directive introduced three years ago. But if you are tired, you are not productive. And if you come back from your holiday absolutely knackered, laptop wearily in hand, what kind of a life is that? This country has reached record levels of burn-out. Not only is this pressure failing to increase productivity, it is destroying the emotional ecology of our lives, the very things which sustain us in being.

There is evidence that this workaholism is literally killing us. Two recent studies have shown that individuals under 45 years of age working more than 48 hours a week have been found to be twice as likely to die from a heart attack compared with those who work less than 40 hours per week.

Commenting on these figures, Jack Dyce, who has done a lot of thinking about the labour market, says: "We ought not to assume that the absence of physical health problems means that all is well. Without seeking to be prescriptive as to what constitutes a 'good life', we may want to argue that a life in which there is no time for recreation, for non-work relationships, for being rather than doing, falls short of the ideal."

One of the few countries which has longer working hours than Britain is America, the land where people are so speeded-up and stressed-out that they scream at the microwave to hurry up. America also happens to have the highest divorce rate in the world. Read my lips – I'll stay with you till the next e-mail. Is nobody out there listening?

Behind all this, in the religious vacuum, a substitute worship is going on. On the high altar stands a golden calf, gleaming in the sunlight. The high-tech pseudo-religious ritual, which demands regular human sacrifice, is orchestrated by some slick global hypnotist-priests in Armani suits. If you can tear off their dark shades, you will find that they have empty eyes.

Oh for some holy days of rest and refreshment, in which we see our world more clearly. It's known as getting a life.

Gary Lewis and the Flying Fairy

S o here I am, sitting in the Phoenix Cinema in Kirkwall, absorbed in the film. It is *Orphans*, Peter Mullan's very black comedy, set in Glasgow. The scenes, especially where west of Scotland bonhomie turns to menace and then violence, are brilliantly observed. I have been there: at funerals and, above all, weddings. The film is absurd, hilarious, and achingly sad.

You know how it is when something is gnawing at you, and you're not quite sure exactly what is going on? On this occasion, it is to do with the leading actor: there is something vaguely familiar about him, about his face and his voice. Who is he? My mind vainly reels through films I've seen, searching the memory traces.

Then, as so often happens with these things, a name suddenly pops up weeks later, unbidden. I've discovered so many times that the gifts from the unconscious mind only come when you're not concentrating on the search. Gary Stevenson. Could it be him?

I'd last seen Gary about 25 years ago, when he was a teenager. He lived along the road from me in Easterhouse. I make some enquiries about the names of the actors in *Orphans*. No Gary Stevenson. But there is a Gary Lewis. It is when I am visiting a friend from Easterhouse days that my hunch is finally confirmed. I am thrilled, especially as I recall how it had all come about.

In the seventies, Easterhouse had a male unemployment rate of around 60per cent. Job creation schemes were all the rage; they were stop-gap measures, designed to give people, especially young people, a chance of employment. Everyone knew it wasn't the answer, but it did at least give despairing people something to get out of their beds for. Some of us who were involved in the community made an application for funding, and a little drama project, which became the Easterhouse Festival, was established. Some very talented people signed up. Robert Robson, a drama school graduate, came on board. Freddy Anderson, a highly creative local writer was engaged. One or two successful productions were followed by the premiere of a new play by Freddy. Called *Krassivy*, it was about the Scottish socialist leader, John McLean. But who could fill the leading role?

Gary Stevenson, that's who. He had never acted in his life. He turned out to be a natural. His performance was passionate, brilliant. Confidence was high, and it was decided that it was time for Easterhouse to take on Edinburgh. The play won the *Scotsman* trophy for the best play on the Festival Fringe. I was pleased for Gary. His parents, Chick and Mary Stevenson, were people I admired.

So here I am, back again in the Phoenix Cinema in Kirkwall. I'm looking forward to the film, the much-lauded *Billy Elliot*. It's the story of a boy from a mining community, at the time of the miners' strike in the eighties, who wants to be a ballet dancer. His wishes are opposed by his gritty, macho, widowed Scottish father, a strike-leading miner who doesn't want any son of his growing up as a flying fairy. The film centres around the relationship between the two, as the father slowly relents and allows his son to develop his God-given talent.

We see the boy on the screen. Then his father. I almost fall off my seat. Gary Stevenson. I had no idea he was in it. He does the role to perfection. He walks down the road with that bravado Glasgow walk I have seen so often – inner sense of inadequacy masked by swaggering "What daur meddle wi' me?"

Afterwards, I phone Chick. This warm and humane socialist is still battling away, campaigning on the issue of pensions. I dial Gary in Italy, where he is working on a film. He is the same as ever. His passionate left wing convictions are still there, his John McLean touch. New Labour is not the top of his personal pops. He is also distrustful of the celebrity culture, and only does media interviews when he has to. His feet are still on the ground.

I think of Robert Robson, who went on to become director of Glasgow's Mayfest. I think of Freddy Anderson of Garthamlock, one of Glasgow's finest writers. Here is a task for the Scottish parliament: provide the political and economic structures within Scotland which allow the Billy Elliots to rise, the Gary Stevensons to flourish. The talent is out there; it needs to be released.

And now Gary Stevenson, otherwise known as Gary Lewis, has been nominated for a Bafta award for best supporting actor in his role in "Billy Elliot." The Easterhouse boy is up against Oliver Reed and Albert Finney. February 25th is D-day.

Go for it, Gary. Show them.

Gordon Brown's Black Friday

Tomorrow, the Rt. Hon Dr Gordon Brown MP, chancellor of the exchequer, Member of the Privy Council, will do something both simple and terrible. Setting aside the great offices of state, he, with his wife Sarah, will take what Orcadian women would call his 'peedie scrap o' a bairn' and ritually place her beyond time.

The event is likely to take place in Fife – the place where Jennifer Jane lived most of her short but precious life. It is where Gordon spent much of his youth. It is the place he represents in Westminster. It is where he and Sarah were married, and where he lives when he is not being the fierce, brooding Iron Chancellor in Downing Street. For Gordon Brown, Fife is home.

Today I feel the strength of these common roots. But I also know where Gordon Brown is 'coming from' in a different sense. Brown also has deep roots in the Christian Socialist movement in Scotland; indeed, he is its leading philosopher and exponent.

I have observed how Gordon has kept true to his Christian convictions, without flaunting them. His political leadership of the international movement to deal with crippling Third World debt has come straight from faith convictions shaped in a manse in Kirkcaldy.

They say that Brown is an ambitious man, with designs

on even higher office. I have no reason to disbelieve that. What I have witnessed, though, is his unambiguous commitment to improve the lot of disadvantaged people, and the clever way in which he has put in place measures to promote this. I would like to see him do much more in this line, but that is by the by. I want to think about tomorrow, which is another day altogether.

Baby Jennifer Jane's sad death is a crisis not just for a prime minister in waiting, but for two human beings. It is one thing to be inspired by Christianity to work for justice for the poorest for the world, quite another to hold on to faith when the new and shining light of your life is cruelly snuffed out. Singing hymns about life after death in church on an ordinary Sunday is quite different from holding a tiny coffin and asking where the hell God is. In more dramatic circumstances, Rod Mayor, husband of the murdered teacher Gwen Mayor, asked: "Where was God when Thomas Hamilton was heading towards Dunblane? Was God on a tea break?"

In his novel *The Blood of the Lamb* Peter de Vries tells the story of a man whose marriage has broken up. He has a beloved young daughter. His life falls apart when little Carol becomes ill, and leukaemia is diagnosed.

On hospital visits, his routine is to go into a nearby Catholic Church and kneel before a crucifix to pray for his daughter's life. On her eighth birthday, he takes along a cake which he has baked. When he gets to the hospital, he finds that Carol is worsening, and she dies in his presence.

The man goes back to the little church. He stands before the crucifix, unwraps the birthday cake, smashes it into the face of Christ, and walks out the door.

A friend of mine, George Cunningham, lost his two-year-old son. At the graveside, the minister said to him to accept his son's death as the will of God. "To hell with a God who puts a two year old into the ground!" George shouted. He is now a minister himself in Canada, but that is another story.

I have conducted a number of funerals of babies and children. They are terrible services to take. I have seen broken young parents and devastated grandparents, some of them regular churchgoers, stand helplessly in bewilderment and grief. I have never, ever been able to utter the words that this is the will of God. I have no explanations to offer, tempting though it may be to fill the gap with babble. When the gods are silent, says Robert Funk, man becomes a gossip.

And yet, when I have stood at these bleak gravesides, a conviction has never failed to rise up within me that this is not the end of the story. Is all this just wishful thinking? Is it just church-fuelled fantasy, a manic whistling in the dark? Perhaps.

The elusive now-you-see-him-now-you-don't God doesn't seem to major on explanations, though plenty of his representatives are more than willing to fill the vacuum. On my best days, though, I hold to the faith that God is a God of promises and unexpected epiphanies.

Gordon and Sarah Brown now face a dark Friday. There was another black Friday, a day of such grievous injustice that even the angels wept. There hung a man with spittle – and icing from a birthday cake? – on his face. By an impossible miracle of grace, that day is now known as Good Friday.

I know very little about life after death. The promise is that every tear will be wiped from every eye, by hands with nailprints on them. God has a lot to answer for, and maybe he will.

And I do believe that Jennifer Jane Brown, and all the other peedie scraps o' bairns so grievously cut short, are not lost to the silent memory of God: for them the singing will never be done.

Tony Blair: St Francis of Assisi or Double-glazing Salesman?

A well known preacher received plaudits from the congregation on the quality of his sermon. When the beadle went up to the pulpit after the service, the preacher's notes were still there. Written in bold capitals beside one passage in the sermon were the words, "Shout louder! Argument weak at this point."

It could have come straight from the sermon notes of the Reverend Tony Blair. In his homilies to the nation, the increasingly strained Vicar of St Albion cranks up the rhetoric at the weakest points in his argument. It's fascinating to observe how the prime minister goes into revivalist mode when the evidence is thinnest. Words like 'evil' and 'monster' fill the airwaves, spoken with burning, intense, conviction. It seems almost a sin to doubt this patently sincere, anguished man who is wearing himself to a shadow on our behalf.

But doubt we must. Tony Blair, that cross between Saint Francis of Assisi and a double-glazing salesman, should not be taken at face value. He is a good man who cannot bear a searchlight on the insecure roots of his own messianic projections. That means that he is at his most dangerous when he is most blazingly sincere.

And he is a Christian believer. So is George W. Bush.

When these two men pray together, I tremble. What they are about to do is certainly not in the name of the churches of this land. Nor is it in the name of many Christians in the United States of America.

Yesterday, the Rev. Alan McDonald, convener of the Kirk's Church and Nation Committee, was at work at Capitol Hill, Washington, as the chosen representative of UK churches, briefing Congressmen on the reservations of the mainline churches of Britain about the forthcoming invasion of Iraq.

I have known Alan McDonald for many years. A former lawyer, he is a fine minister and a very able thinker. On his visit, Alan will learn something of the struggles of the churches in America over the war issue. On this side of the water, the impression is often given that American Christianity is solely represented by rabid right-wing fundamentalism. This is far from the truth.

The mainline churches in USA are at the heart of the opposition to this war. Post-September 11 America is a difficult place in which to minister with integrity today, because there is such hurt, and an understandable desire for retaliatory action.

Accusations of lack of patriotism fly around. Friends have told me of one clergy couple who were dismissed by their congregation because they raised concerns about the war. One assistant priest was pushed away from the microphone by her boss as she said prayers, and the congregation began chanting "USA! USA!"

Patriotism is not enough. America is a great land with a love of freedom at its heart, and we, in this country, are natural allies. The hard truth, though, is that the moral case for this war has not been made in a way that the Christian churches can support it.

If the main aim is to disarm a despot, then the weapons inspectors need to be given proper support to complete the process. If the object is to remove a tyrant who kills his own people, we must ask why Robert Mugabe sleeps bliss-fully in his bed at night. If the purpose is international justice and a new, fairer, world order, questions have to be asked as to why the west has armed and supported the "monsters" Saddam and bin Laden, and why the same energy is not going into resolving the Palestinian issue.

There are serious, troubling, questions about the after-math of a war which will make not just widows, but mar-tyrs. Douglas Hurd – no raving radical he – correctly ob-serves that "this war may be won in six days, but lost in six months".

In terms of Christian theology, the current proposals far from satisfy the criteria for a just war. That is why so many church members, many of whom have never demonstrated before, have taken to the streets. This column can reveal that the next Moderator, Professor Iain Torrance, took part in the Glasgow march. What is particularly significant about this is that Professor Torrance was, until recently, convener of the Kirk's Forces Chaplains. Many chaplains are disturbed by this war.

The churches have no monopoly of wisdom. The job of spiritual leaders, though, is to measure the actions of the government of the day against religious values. (That is why Archbishop Conti's recommendation to "trust the prime minister" – in contrast to the guidance issued by Cardinal Cormac Murphy-O'Connor in England – feels more like an abdication of spiritual leadership on a critical national issue than the act of a trail-blazer.)

Today, a fearless leader will be enthroned at Canterbury. He will both support and defy the prime minister. The truth is that, despite much sweat and evangelical earnest-ness, Tony Blair has lost the moral and religious argument. No more can shouting louder cover up the weakness of his case. As a Christian man, he must consider the fearful possibility that even God might be saying, "Not in my name".

Save us from Holy Newspeak

Welcome to new soap opera week. *River City*, which follows the lives of residents in a close-knit Glasgow community made its debut on Tuesday. Another potboiler, which might be called *Edinburgh Pulp Fiction*, has been running all week at the Church of Scotland's headquarters at 121 George Street. Set in a building which looks like a cross between a grand Victorian public toilet and the Edwardian headquarters of a national bank, it tells of the relationships between everyday ecclesiastical urban folk.

The story line is this: how did it come to be that the church of John Knox, worrier of Mary Queen of Scots, pulped a magazine because it contained some fairly mild criticisms of a prince of the land? *Edinburgh Pulp Fiction* is a grubby, low-life tale of inflated power, intrigue, virtual censorship, spindoctoring, waste of money, and cover-up: and all at the highest levels of the church.

When I first heard that the Kirk had ordered that 50,000 copies of *Life & Work* be pulped, at a cost of £17,000, I had assumed that for such radical action to be taken, the article must be seriously defamatory. Having read the dreaded piece in full, I can report that, wonder upon wonder, I have been neither corrupted nor offended by it.

One church spokesperson rubbished the article by saying that it had been commissioned from a free-lance journalist, and its tone was "not appropriate for the Church of Scotland". The truth is that the writer was John Lloyd, one of the most distinguished commentators in Britain, and had first appeared in the *New Statesman,* without any reaction whatsoever.

Rosemary Goring, the editor of *Life & Work,* felt it would be a good piece to use. I agree with her judgment. Lloyd's piece is insightful, witty, and, indeed, understanding of the prince. But for the church mandarins, anxious about their relationship with St James's Palace, it was all too dangerous. Get the shredder out.

For some strange reason, the presbyterian punters in the pew had to be protected from a well-written, thoughtful article which was already in the public domain. Thou shalt not cause even the mildest flutter in the royal doocot seemed to be the eleventh commandment.

The desire not to cause even the slightest offence to the great and the good showed the Kirk at its sycophantic worst. Pressure was applied to drop the offending article. There were hints that if it appeared, church headquarters would have to disassociate itself from it (Jings! Crivvens! Helpmaboab!) – even though every issue of *Life & Work* carries a disclaimer making clear that the views expressed in the magazine are not necessarily the official views of the Kirk.

The pulping was hushed up. Not a word of this was reported to the ballsachingly boring, carefully managed General Assembly in May. It is scandalous that the church should act in this craven and secret manner.

One of the problems of a 'national' church is that it can produce too many grovellers in high places. Cosy, flattering little conversations at St Andrews House or Buckingham Palace can have a corrupting influence. The effects are evidenced not in open forums, but in whispers in corridors or remarks over sherry.

There is another troubling issue. Rosemary Goring, by doing away with tedious church 'insider-speak' and commissioning good writers to address contemporary issues, attracted new readers and increased sales. But some men and women in suits felt that the magazine should be primarily a mouthpiece for the committees of the church.

All this is bad enough. The rest is worse. When the story about the pulping broke at the weekend, the consequent nauseous church spindoctoring was worthy of New Labour at its most obnoxious. Of course Ms Goring hadn't been pressurised. No, no, the Principal Clerk's office would not seek to influence the contents of *Life & Work*. Wouldn't dream of such a thing. Rosemary Goring was even congratulated on her bravery for pulping the magazine in the face of pressure!

George Orwell, where are you now that we need you? God save us from Holy Newspeak. We are asked to believe that as outstanding a journalist as Rosemary Goring suddenly woke up in the middle of the night and decided, without pressure, to pulp the freshly printed magazine. Give us a break. This is Alice in Wonderland stuff.

The truth is that Rosemary Goring – now, understandably, former editor – was subjected to what she called 'uncomfortable and fierce' pressures, and was even told that she might be 'ostracised' at 121 George Street. Charming. She added that the pressure was "a revealing example of the fearful flexing of the Church's corporate muscle. The decision to pulp the magazine was nothing less than censorship."

There are many good people in 121 George Street. Some of them are sickened by this covert, unaccountable use of power. They say that critics are rubbished and characters are assassinated in whispers over coffee. All in a Christian way, of course.

So the soap opera runs, and runs. It would be hilarious,

if it weren't so sad. What is clear is this: if the Kirk is to be reformed, it needs, more than ever, an independent magazine which tells it like it is. The many committed members of the Kirk deserve no less.

The smooth, butter-wouldn't-melt-in-the-mouth control-freak tendency needs to be told exactly where to go.

Slim Jim: The UnPresbyterian Cowdenbeath Playboy

So the Slim One will be buried from Glasgow Cathedral tomorrow. It's a deliciously ironic thought. It will be a wonderfully quirky historic moment when the unPresbyterian Cowdenbeath playboy, who has had more livers than Rangers have had players sent off this season, is borne aloft from one of Scotland's great religious shrines.

Jim Baxter and I had a lot in common. The same age: both from the same mining community: both left-footed. We competed for the Number 11 shirt at Beath High School. (Surely it was favouritism on the part of the teachers that got Jim the jersey ahead of me?). We both played at Hampden Park. (Jim for Scotland, while I was outside left in the Scottish Clergy Select side against former Rangers and Celtic players. "Now Ferguson sprints past Bobby Shearer," cried the commentator, the estimable Jimmy Currie. At that stage Bobby Shearer was ten feet wide.)

Beath High School, Cowdenbeath, has many famous alumnae, but none as celebrated as Slim Jim. When I first got to know him he was, like myself, skinny and slight. He looked as if a puff of wind would blow him away. In adolescence, he grew – like myself – to be tall, and – how can I put this? – elegant. The handsome Jim was a magnet for sophisticated burdz from as far afield as Lochgelly and Kelty. Like myself, of course.

At that point we did not know that Baxter would strut his stuff on the world football stage. Although Jim was a willowy, wispy character, he was tough as nails, as befits a miner. He signed for Crossgates Primrose, a local junior side, for £50 – and promptly bought his mother a washing machine with the money.

As a local journalist, I used to cover two, or even three, junior football matches in one afternoon for the Sunday papers. These sides were full of hard nuts – I could never understand why the mining clubs all seemed to have such sweet names as 'Primrose' and 'Violet' – and games were marked by vendettas, eye gouging, and knee-in-the-groin warfare. Referees were routinely chased out of town. It was in this atmosphere that the underweight outside left learned to survive.

When Jim signed for Rangers, his weekly wage was £22, with a £3 bonus for a win. He quickly became Scotland's first pop football superstar, and he dressed the part. By now he was attracting not just burdz from Kelty, but glamorous models from all over the known world. He revelled in the high life.

As Baxter reached iconic status, he would bring his mining pals over from Fife to Glasgow, and install them in good hotels. He sent the bills for the outrageous drinking parties to Ibrox – and they were paid. The big-city invasion of the Cowdenbeath playboys is one of the more touching episodes of recent Scottish football history.

The boozing and gambling laid waste to his life. "My lifestyle has cost me my health, and before that my marriage and my kids for a time," he said. "The fact is booze can cost you all the things that are nearest and dearest to you. I've got two choices – I can forget the bevvy sessions, or I can kiss my ass goodbye. It's as simple as that."

I last spoke to Jim a couple of years or so ago, when we were speaking at a European football supporters 'do' in London. He was drinking mineral water. He was in jocular mood, pleased about comments I had written about him in a book about Cowdenbeath, *Black Diamonds and the Blue Brazil*. He joshed me about living in what he laughingly described as the "posh end" of Cowdenbeath – the council houses rather than the miners' rows – and said he hoped the Blue Brazil might win promotion again at some stage.

Some people will be sniffy about Baxter's funeral service being in Glasgow Cathedral, as if people had to pass some moral examination in order to qualify for a church funeral. But no one can see into the heart of another human being. Judgement is God's business. So is grace. My old mucker, Easterhouse boy Stuart MacQuarrie, will conduct the service well.

I want to celebrate the outrageous talent of the best and most elegant footballer I have ever seen. So good was he that the great Pele opined aloud that he wished Jim had been born a Brazilian. But Baxter *was* born a Brazilian – a Blue Brazilian.

By the way, Jim, after Tuesday night's game the Blue Brazil are sitting nervously at the top of the league with three matches to go. If you're anywhere near the angel who takes to do with the Scottish Third Division, put in a wee word from me. And thanks for the memories.

Follow El Shaggo till you saggo

The time has come, the Walrus said, to talk of shagging. (Your actual Walrus didn't say anything about shagging, but you know what I mean.) By shagging, I'm not talking about American line dancing. I'm not talking about carpets. I'm not talking about cormorants. I'm talking about, well, houghmagandie.

The word 'shagging' contains hints of casualness. It's not a term which is redolent with notions of commitment, or any of that kind of romantic stuff; nor are we necessarily talking about great erotic encounters. It's a what-rabbits-do kind of business, part of the human service industry. Getting it on. Doing it. Are we all clear about the subject under discussion?

Shagging is in the air, so to speak. It's everywhere. It's in the language. Some months ago, while treading the streets of Glasgow, I saw that the cinema neon signs were flashing out the name of the film, *The spy who shagged me.* Just the title for the City of Culture. It is a privilege to be alive in such elevated times.

Shagging is pretty well compulsory these days. In fact, it has become an unchallengeable cultural ideology. Anybody who does not have the mandatory 2.6 orgasms a week is regarded as a dangerous deviant. Celibates are liable to be rounded up and sent to re-education camps.

The shagging culture is so pervasive that if I were to write a six-part television series challenging the dominant ideology of shagging, the producers would fill it with shagging scenes to boost the ratings, and would run shagging trailers for the anti-shagging series. There is absolutely no way out of this.

Now casual shagging tends not to be a Presbyterian sport, at least not in public. Nor is it integral to Roman Catholic Church programmes for parish renewal. (There's a story told about a community centre in Australia which advertised a series of talks titled "Sex without guilt", while across the road the Catholic Church was running seminars on "Guilt without sex".)

In the patriarchal period of the Old Testament, one of the gods was El Shaddai, the god of the mountains. In the modern pantheon, one of the key gods is El Shaggo. (There is an illusion around at the moment that we live in a non-religious age. This is not so: it is just that the objects of devotion have changed.) In the post-modern age, no god is pre-eminent, of course, and they're all entitled to their 15 minutes of fame. Not only are they all relative, they're all relatives.

Up there with El Shaggo is his divine pal El Shoppo, whose gleaming temples, teeming with worshippers, can be found in all modern cities. Making up this dominant unholy trinity is Mand-El, the god of hype and bullshit, who has visited us grateful mortals for a season in the person of his blessed son, Peter. Mand-El acts as divine spin doctor for El Shaggo and El Shoppo; it was he who was responsible for their marketing slogans "Follow El Shoppo till you droppo", and "Follow El Shaggo until you saggo". Mand-El also designed their celestial websites, and he publishes the pantheon's magazine, Hell-O.

The pantheon changes all the time, with various B-celeb gods jostling for position. The nearest to a supreme god is the Olympian Narcissus, who inhabits the heavenly hall of mirrors.

The greatest philosopher of shagging is not Dr Alex Comfort, but the 19th century German thinker Arthur Schopenhauer. The melancholy Schaggenhauer *(Schome mischtake schurely? – Ed.)* is your man for the shagging. His view is that human beings are primarily driven by the will to survive and reproduce, and all this stuff about romance is simply Nature's intellectual and emotional foreplay for what is the only serious game in town – the survival of the species.

It's important to keep the whole shagging business in proportion, since El Shaggo has always been around, doing his bit for evolution. The difference today, though, is that El Shaggo, backed by the omnipresent Mand-El, demands total and unquestioning obedience. Anyone who questions his divine credentials is liable to be locked in the cultural stocks and ridiculed.

What is not highlighted, of course, is that the pressures of the obligatory shagging culture – backed by unlimited hype – move young people into sex before they are emotionally ready for it. Fact: in the past five years, the incidence of sexually transmitted diseases has increased by more than 35 per cent in Scotland. Fact: heterosexually-transmitted Aids is on the increase in this country. Fact: despite the public awareness of contraception, teenage pregnancies and abortions are increasing. The dark side of the shagging culture masks emotional wreckage, unwanted children and the slaughter of the innocents.

By the way, the god you see sitting in the corner, weeping, is the god of small children.

I'd Rather be a Darkie than a Tim

A h, but the past is another country: unless you live in Scotland, that is. On Saturday, bedecked tribes will gather in solemn assembly at our national shrine. During an afternoon of ritual and worship, a huge congregation will celebrate ancient mysteries, Hymns will be sung. Heroes of old, mythic, religious wars will be lauded.

After – or even during – this gigantic *Songs of Praise*, which will be shown on television screens around the world, human blood will be shed. The God at the heart of this theatre of worship is a demanding idol, one who insists, apparently, upon human sacrifices.

Yes, Saturday is cup final day, the greatest occasion in Scotland's national football calendar. It ought to be a wonderful day out for families, a celebration of all that's good about the game. It won't. After all, this is Scotland.

What will happen is that a team which includes several Roman Catholic foreign mercenaries (Rangers) will be howled on by a frenzied group of supporters singing anti-Catholic songs. The other team (Celtic), mainly Protestant, will be backed by rabid fans singing anti-Protestant songs.

The Rangers supporters – decked out in blue, white and red – will all be singing from the same hymn sheet, so to speak. How about these beautifully crafted lyrics:

Hail, hail the Pope's in jail.

Or how about the lovely: *We're up to our knees in Fenian blood, surrender or you'll die.*

At the other end of the ground, the green-white-yellow-draped Celtic choristers will respond with the charming *When the music stops, fuck King Billy and John Knox.*

And that's only for starters. It gets much worse, but you don't want to go there. If you really must, there are lots of web sites designed to satisfy every taste.

None of this is new, of course. That is the problem. Let me take you back a mere 15 years. A friend of mine organized a bus trip for Pakistani and Indian youngsters resident in Glasgow. On the way home, there was an outbreak of singing. My friend was stunned by what he heard.

"I'd rather be a darkie than a Tim", one group roared, to the tune of Simon and Garfunkel's "I'd rather be a hammer than a nail".

These dark-skinned young Rangers supporters were bawling out the statement that being a 'Tim' (a Roman Catholic) was so bad that they would even prefer to be a 'darkie'. They were oblivious to the fact that what they were singing was deeply insulting to their own ancestry.

And these pro-Protestant, anti-Catholic youngsters were Muslims and Hindus! Eh? Welcome to the joyous, convoluted world of west of Scotland sectarianism.

Back to the cup final. As the hate-filled hymns cascade down from the state-of-the-art stands and the tension transmits itself to the players, it might be assumed that the choirs are made up of bitter people involved in the Irish troubles. Some are, as the flags and the mini buses in the parking lot testify. But mouthing the words will also be

Scottish lawyers and bank managers and accountants. To pretend that it's all down to inarticulate neanderthals is to live in a state of denial.

Sectarianism is a blight upon the new Scotland. It is a gaping wound in the body civic. For too long, it has been regarded as a 'given' of Scottish life. The time for surgery for this debilitating sickness is now.

The Old Firm clashes are neither the cause of sectarianism nor its only poisonous manifestation, but the divisive, high-profile symbolism is so potent that until it is tackled, nothing serious can be done.

Ah, say the defenders, it's only football songs. Boys will be boys. Why make a fuss about something so trivial? But those who argue that Old Firm matches are substitutes for war, and therefore healthier, turn their heads away from what is actually happening in the casualty rooms at Glasgow's hospitals. And if you are wearing the wrong colours in the wrong place at the wrong time, you may end up dead.

Why is hate-filled sectarianism not treated with the seriousness now afforded racism? Let me give you an example. At an Old Firm match soon after September 11, a Celtic fan notoriously made an aeroplane gesture in the direction of Rangers' American midfielder Claudio Reyna. The culprit was identified from video film, and banned from Celtic Park. People guilty of racist chants are rightly ejected from Scottish football grounds.

Will the singers of songs of murderous sectarian hatred be similarly dealt with? Of course not. Why? Because they might have to clear half the ground. And it wouldn't do to shame the middle classes, would it? This hypocrisy runs right to the highest levels of our national life.

Here is another factor which dares not speak its name.

Rangers and Celtic benefit from bigotry, while officially deploring it. The supporters who sing the songs and buy the merchandise keep the clubs' coffers full.

There is only one solution. If Rangers and Celtic will not voluntarily embark on a programme of banning troublemakers – and they won't, despite having the technology – then the Old Firm games should be played behind closed doors.

Will our craven, complicit authorities take this necessary action? Don't hold your breath.

Questions posed by an orphaned, armless, Muslim boy

A picture has haunted me all week. It was in Monday's *Herald*, under the heading "Can you help me get my arms back?" A 12-year-old boy, Ali Ismaeel Abbas was lying on his back, cruciform-style. His arms were bleeding, bandaged stumps. His torso was covered in terrible burns. It is an image that can only be viewed through tears.

The Iraqi boy was fast asleep when the missile landed on the shack his family lived in. His father, his five months pregnant mother, and his brother were all killed. So were his aunt, three cousins, and three other relatives.

Ali was the 'lucky' one. His arms were blasted off. Lying in the overwhelmed Kindi Hospital in Baghdad, his body was covered by a cage, in order to keep the bedclothes from contact with his seared flesh. A surviving aunt was at his bedside, feeding him, washing him, and repeatedly telling him his parents had gone to heaven.

"Can you help me get my arms back?" asked the tearful Ali. "Do you think the doctors can get me another pair of hands? If I don't get a pair of hands, I will commit suicide." He has been shocked and awed. I guess Ali should be excused from attendance at the liberation street parties.

The official term for Ali Ismaeel Abbas is 'collateral damage.' Yet neutral, value-free techno-speak is totally inadequate in talking about this atrocity. We need to ransack the outer reaches of human vocabulary to try to find terms which can even begin to do justice to such a personal tragedy.

Another image I have before me is of a tank, with the word 'Apocalypse' painted on its side. Driving it is a helmeted young man, confident in the overwhelming power and advanced technology he represents. The stars and stripes, insignia of the undisputed global emperor, fly from the vehicle. Old Glory. He will go home soon, to be feted (rightly) for his bravery. But through the night, he may well be haunted by questions and images. That is what it means to be a human being.

Sometimes it is necessary to go to war, to defend your family and your community against the aggressor. It can be done with moral integrity only as an unavoidable last resort, when all else has failed. Once the dogs of war are unleashed, the consequences cannot be controlled, even when precautions are taken – and the coalition forces have been doing their best – to avoid civilian casualties.

It looks like Saddam Hussein has avoided accountability to the international human community, but he may find himself naked before Allah. George Bush and Tony Blair will likewise have their day in an ultimate court which cannot be rigged. They will be invited to prove that their hands are as clean as the white hats they wear. No spin doctors will be permitted to put a gloss on things.

God, how I am heart-sick of the lies of this war.

The talk is of technology and victory, and on which country is next in the firing line. But many kinds of collateral damage still need to be addressed, before moving on. James Morris, the United Nations Food Agency's executive director, told the security council yesterday that they were $1bn short of the sum it needed for emergency food in Africa.

Food shortages threaten 14 million in Ethiopia, 7 million in Zimbabwe, 3.2 million in Malawi, 2.9 million in Sudan, 2.7 million in Zambia, 1.9 million in Angola, 1 million in Eritrea, as well as millions more in Swaziland, Lesotho, Mozambique, Uganda, Congo, Democratic Republic of Congo, and the western Sahel.

Mr Morris contrasted the British and US governments' pledges to feed Iraqis with evaporating concern for Africa. "As much as I don't like it, I cannot escape the thought that we have a double standard." His view was backed by Carol Bellamy, director of Unicef, the UN children's fund, in Johannesburg. "I am very concerned, because the world's attention is so focused on Iraq, that from Afghanistan to South Africa, funding for these real ongoing crises could be put in jeopardy," she said.

Can we expect regime change in Zimbabwe, where a vicious dictator is oppressing his people? Nah. Of course not. It's the fossil fuels, stupid. Will we have a coalition of the willing which will tackle world poverty and environmental damage, establish a court of International Justice at which war criminals will be tried – regardless of country – and invest in non-violent programmes for conflict resolution, all backed by the kind of bottomless 'war chests' which are conjured up miraculously and instantaneously? Holding of the breath is not necessary.

Meanwhile, in a land redolent of biblical names, the apparatus of an evil tyrant is dismantled – and last night's scenes of rejoicing showed how much Saddam was hated – even as a global empire makes further plans to extend its hegemony. The end result may be the apocalypse flagged up on the all-conquering tank.

Addiction to affluence and power is the Babylonian captivity of our day, as countless children die of starvation. And in a hospital in Iraq, a grotesque Good Friday image of an orphaned, armless, Muslim boy poses profound questions for victors and vanquished alike. Forgive us, Father, for we know what we are doing.

Beware of Vikings Bearing Gifts

So what did the Vikings give us? Rape, pillage, red hair, freckles, multiple sclerosis, and now, it seems, some forms of cancer. One thing for sure: when you saw the Scandinavian longships on the horizon, you knew it wasn't the Sunday School picnic arriving. It was prudent to beware of Vikings bearing gifts.

It emerged yesterday that Vikings who raided or settled in north-east Scotland in the Middle Ages left a legacy of cancer in the local population. Scientists revealed that breast and ovarian cancers in clinics in Dundee and Aberdeen share a genetic origin with cancers common in Scandinavia.

The authorized Viking version is that they came to Scotland in peace and friendship. Here's what really happened. Alleging that Orkney had weapons of mass destruction, they decided to liberate the people, secure the oil terminal, and institute regime change. After a bit of shock-and-awe involving axes and stuff, they set up Orkney Islands Council – consisting of glove puppets – and appointed the legendary Jo 'The Beast' Grimond as warlord. He was succeeded by his fearsome lovechild, Jimbo 'Bloodaxe' Wallace, who instituted the notorious Orkney Reign of Terror. People still speak of it in whispers.

As for weapons of mass destruction, the rockets that were said to be pointing at Bergen turned out to be ancient standing stones. The only things the Viking weapons inspectors found were old axes which they had sold to the Orcadians in the first place but, hey, who cares? Then the hairy giants with the horns on their heads said to Shetland: "What are you grinning at? You're next, pal."

After that, the cheery Vikings swarmed over parts of Scotland, toppling statues, installing Ebbe 'The Berserk' Skovdhal in Aberdeen, interacting with flower-throwing natives and giving people red hair, freckles and doses of the clap. It was a cultural exchange, sponsored by the Oslo Arts Council.

Researchers for a BBC documentary recently established that people from, or living in, Orkney, Shetland and the far north, with red hair, fair skin and freckles are almost certainly Vikings. Red hair, fair skin and freckles? That's the electronic crofterina. The other reason I know that my wife is a Viking is that she tries to resolve minor domestic disputes by chopping off my heid. I've been dodging the swinging axe for 36 years now, which makes the electronic crofter one of the fittest men in the north.

The Vikings do get a bit of an unfair press, though. Their reputation for raping, pillaging and all sorts of unPresbyterian stuff has been highly exaggerated. The historical evidence shows that many of them were peaceable people, forced from their own country through economic hardship to search for land on which to settle. They set out on longships from Scandinavia, and ended up in places like Shetland and Orkney, where they married the locals and farmed the land.

The incomers made good settlers. They did bring good gifts, as well as diseases. Their culture, jewellery, games, seafaring skills, and new ways of curing fish helped to shape modern Orkney. And the blood of the Vikings is still strong in the northern isles.

The BBC research also surprisingly revealed that the Scots were not predominantly Celtic; they had a Saxon/Danish heritage like that of the rest of the UK mainland. A BBC spokesman said: "It looks as if the indigenous Celtic people were ruled by people other than the natives. It's early days, but the survey shows what a mixed heritage we have in the British isles."

The truth is that we Scots are a mongrel nation. All this talk about purity of race is baloney. Sir Iain Noble's talk of preserving Scotland's so-called genetic purity and his 'inordinate pride' in having no English blood in his veins is offensive fantasy.

We are all of us peoples of mixed blood. Unchallenged hatred of incomers can stretch all the way to ethnic cleansing. The ideology of racism is based on a lie which has to be refuted in every generation.

So is the ideology of corporate violence. The same conquering Vikings also gave us Magnus, the gentle saint of Orkney. As a ruling earl in a bloodthirsty age, Magnus knew all about violence. He also understood that human beings had to find ways of resolving disputes other than war.

During a power struggle with his cousin Haakon, Magnus laid down his life for the peace of Orkney. In a passage in the *Orkneyinga Saga* echoing the gospel story, Magnus prayed for forgiveness for his executioner. The date? April 16th, St Magnus Day, the day on which I write this piece.

Tomorrow is Good Friday. A black and terrible deed took place at Golgotha, the place of the skull, where a man laid down his life in love for the world. His disciples, like

Magnus, have things to tell us for our long-term health, even as new plagues of awesome violence are let loose on the world.

There are some Viking gifts worth cherishing. As the medieval Hymn to Saint Magnus puts it:

O Magnus of fame
On the barque of the heroes
On the crest of the waves
On the sea, on the land,
Aid and preserve us.